THE
WIZARD'S
WAY

THE WIZARD'S WAY

*Secrets from Wizards of the Past
Revealed for
the World Changers of Today*

TOBIAS BECKWITH

FIRST EDITION

Section Title Illustrations and Cover Design by Kiva Singh
www.kivasingh.com

Edited by Carolyn Uno (Tigris)
Book design and layout by Tobias Beckwith
www.tobiasbeckwith.com

Library of Congress Cataloging-in-Publication Date has been applied for.
ISBN 0-9779843-8-9

*Dedicated to my mother, Margy C. Beckwith,
who planted the seed for this book long
before I could have ever imagined it myself.*

Table of Contents

Contents

Creative vs. Reactive   95

Radical Responsibility   117

The Wizard as Renegade   131

The Art of Persuasion ... 213

Preface

Preface

*A journey is like marriage. The certain way to be wrong
is to think you control it.*

-- John Steinbeck[1]

This is a book for all of us who, after receiving what we thought was a good education, whether that meant graduating from high school, college, or graduate school, found ourselves struggling to succeed in the real world. It is for all who want to be more effective, potent agents of change and wonder why their less thoughtful, less educated peers are succeeding, leading companies, and making effective change in the world when we seem unable to. It is for those like me, who wondered why the wonderful education we worked so hard for had failed to teach us the basics we needed to achieve the kind of success we had expected.

This book is derived from my own experiences and observations over the past 40 years since I graduated from college. It contains many of the lessons I've learned from teaching students and clients to be better performers and from managing various show business enterprises, as well as the secrets I've learned from spending 25 years working with some of the world's top magicians.

This is actually the second version of this book I've written. After completing the first version, I read what I had written and realized there was a great deal missing. I had lots of empowering techniques but no clear understanding of the core characteristics that set the true wizard apart from everyone else. So I went back and read biographies of those I believed to be true wizards, re-read the legends and stories of Merlyn, Gandalf, and the rest. I had long conversations with people I know who either are true wizards themselves or share my interest in the subject. And I did a lot of thinking. The book in your hands is the result of that re-thinking.

My hope is that what you learn here will inspire you and provide the basic information you need to begin your own transformation and join me on the path to wisdom, power, and freedom—the wizard's way.

Notes:

1.	Steinbeck, John. *Travels with Charley in Search of America*, page 1.

Introduction

Introduction

I will tell you something else, King, which may be a surprise for you. It will not happen for hundreds of years, but both of us are to come back.

—Merlyn, from *The Once & Future King*[1]

Whether or not you know it, you have the potential to be a real wizard. Our times, like those inhabited by King Arthur and his advisor, the wizard Merlyn, are times of transition and transformation. These are times that cry out for us to claim our birthright as men and women of wisdom, of action, to claim and exercise our natural powers as true wizards.

Wizards?

Who does not know what a wizard is? We all know about Merlyn, Gandalf, Dumbledore—wise old men with white beards and pointed caps, poring over their giant books or gazing into crystal balls. They all perform feats of magic and have access to secret knowledge and unseen realms. And they live in storybooks. Surely that is what a wizard is! What more does anyone need to know? Why would anyone write a whole book about wizards?

Let's look a bit deeper and ask a few more questions: Is there such a thing as a real wizard? Do wizards have to be old? Or male? What is the purpose of a wizard? Where do wizards come from? And given that Hogwarts School is a fiction, how does one learn to be a wizard? What does a wizard know that you don't? Does being a wizard require certain unique talents? If you met a wizard, how would you know that he or she was a wizard?

These are some of the questions.

And the answers? I have good news and bad news for you in that department.

The good news: I've found some of the answers, and you can read them in the pages that follow. However (this is the bad news), you won't find all the answers here. Part of becoming a real wizard is learning how to learn from experience. Your most important lessons will be the ones you learn firsthand, from your own experiences. Those lessons won't come from this book or any other.

Even though I cannot give you all the knowledge you will need to become a real wizard, I can guide you to a path of discovery so that you will be able to answer these and many more questions about what it is to be a wizard for yourself. Having been on this path myself for some time now, I can tell you that it is exciting, sometimes leading to the heights of ecstasy and enlightenment. At times it is also a bit frightening and difficult, because it requires you to give up ideas and beliefs you may hold dear. If you choose this path, you will find your senses re-awakening to the wonders around you, and you will enjoy taking a more active and effective role in the world around you. Perhaps, like Merlyn, you will even find that you look more youthful as you consciously re-awaken and integrate mind, body, and spirit into a more powerful way of being. All this and much more await those with the curiosity and daring to embark on the wizard's way.

Why, you might ask, is daring required? Why can't you just have the benefits and freedoms that come with a wizard's powers? What could be so scary about becoming a wizard? The answers lie ahead; but here are some hints. With power comes responsibility. Real responsibility frightens many of us. Most of us spend much of our lives assuming that real power is "out there" somewhere and is not our personal responsibility. We assume there is some amorphous, huge "they" out there somewhere who make all the big decisions and hold the real power—and that our very small "me" has very little power. It can be easier to live without all that responsibility. It is much easier to do things the way we've always done them and follow the rules "they" have laid down for us. It takes courage and energy to accept that "they" only have the power that "I" give them. A wizard has to have the courage to take back her own power and to take much more responsibility for herself and the world around her than the everyday citizen does.

While there are wizards who seek knowledge and power only for themselves (in stories, they are called "evil wizards"), my interest here is in recruiting good wizards. A good wizard is one who uses the power and freedom he gains to help empower and enlighten those around him and to create a better world for all. Good wizards like to help others along the path to true wizardry!

The other reason that it requires courage to travel the wizard's path is that wizards seek out secret knowledge, which is often forbidden knowledge. Forbidden paths are generally forbidden for a reason (sometimes a good reason and sometimes just because those who take the path might disrupt or inconvenience those in power). Whatever the reason, there is a price to pay for taking a forbidden path. It is wise to know that price before undertaking any journey into the secret realms.

Why Wizards?

We need wizards today. We need wise and powerful people who can think and act in ways that will make our world a beautiful and exciting place for ourselves and for our children. Technology and industry have combined to bring us to a turning point. On one hand, we have the ability to destroy our world many times over and make it uninhabitable for humans—a burned-out garbage dump, a mere shell of a planet that once held great potential. On the other hand, we have the technology that, if used wisely and carefully, can create an amazing and exciting green future in which humans, animals, and plants thrive, progress, and perhaps even embark on a journey to the stars. The true wizards among us will guide the planet on its journey in one direction or the other. Our potential is limitless—if we don't kill ourselves off before we reach it.

So this is your invitation to become one of the good wizards, taking your own and the planet's fate into your hands. You can choose to join the adventure as a player, or you can just go along for the ride, keeping fingers and toes crossed that those who have chosen the wizard's path will be wise enough to make the right decisions.

How This Book Came to Be

This book actually originated with something my mother told me many, many years ago (when I was 17, I think). I had just finished reading a book on acting—*An Actor Prepares* by Constantin Stanislavsky. Mom wanted to read it, too, though I couldn't think why. I knew that I wanted to be an actor, but I was sure she had no such aspirations. Anyway, she read the book and, to my surprise, really enjoyed it. We talked about much of what the book had to say, and one of the things she told me has remained with me ever since: "The ideas he gives for being a better actor would be really useful for anyone." I think she was right. Learning to act the part of an effective human being can teach us to actually become such a person.

Since then, I have put a version of that idea to use many, many times. I've used ideas and techniques I learned while studying acting, voice, dance, and, later, magic, kriya yoga, and other skills in ways that those who created them probably never imagined. I am convinced that the results have given me a confidence and level of effectiveness in social relationships and in business that I never would have experienced without them. I continue to learn each time I use them myself or teach them to others.

I have taught these skills to businesspeople and magicians, to scientists and college students. I have used what I learned to counsel friends who felt somehow stuck in one aspect of their lives or another. They felt trapped in unrewarding jobs or bad relationships— things most of us have experienced at one time or another—and they needed the ability to see how they were trapping themselves by playing a particular role they had created for themselves. Once they realized they had the ability to re-write the role, they could move on.

Magicians and Wizardry

The story of wizardry is inextricably bound up with the story of magic, and magic is certainly a large part of the path that led me to study wizards.

Magic has been a lifelong fascination for me. I am sure I must have encountered the idea of magic in fairy tales my parents told me, but my first clear memory of it comes from an experience I had in first grade. Having just learned to read, my classmates and I were given the opportunity to buy a book for the very first time. The books offered were from a series, each with the title "The First Book of ___." There was The *First Book of Farming*, *The First Book of Origami*, and so on. There must have been 30 or 40 titles in all. Somewhere in the middle of the list, I found *The First Book of Magic*. Impossible! How could it be so easy to find out about the secret art of magic? I raised my hand and got my teacher to come over. In a whisper, I asked her, "Will this book really teach me magic?" She said yes, so I eagerly put in my order. I was amazed that I was the only one in the class to order that book. What could the others have been thinking, ordering mundane books on baseball, making dolls, or caring for pets when they had a chance to discover the closely guarded secrets of magic?

I went home, and for days I imagined what it was going to be like to work magic. I would wave a hand at the sky and command the rain to begin or end, depending on my mood. I imagined muttering a secret spell that would give me the power to run even faster than my best friend, who always beat me when we ran footraces. I would snap my fingers and turn back time when Mom and Dad had decided it was time for me to go to bed, but I still felt like staying up to play. That book could not arrive fast enough to suit me!

Finally, the books arrived. It was the end of the school day, and our teacher had each of us open the box our book came in. I peered into the box, and there it was—a beautiful hardcover book with a yellow dust jacket. In big, bold black letters was printed

The First Book
of
MAGIC

Our teacher had us take out our books and then showed us how to properly open a new book. She showed us how to turn each page and run our hand down the inside of the page so that later it would open easily without cracking the spine. I hated having my book out on the desk where everyone could see it. I was to be the only special one with magic powers, and I feared they would all want my book, with its extraordinary secrets—but no one seemed to notice. I closed the book and put it away in its box and then into my book bag. That day, I went straight home from school and closed myself in my room.

I sat on my bed and opened the box to take out the book, carefully, as our teacher had showed us. On the first page, I read the magician's oath: "Never reveal the secrets of magic!" Yes! I knew these secrets were not meant for everyone. I repeated the oath to myself several times, feeling that by doing so, I was joining the great secret brotherhood of wizards. I was certain I had taken the first step toward acquiring the real powers that magic would bring me, and I was ready for that power.

Ever since my parents had disappointed me by promising me a brother, someone to be my companion and playmate, and then brought home a mere baby in diapers, I had been yearning for more power.

I had expected a big brother who would teach me things and play with me all day. Instead, this tiny, bawling pink thing came home and stole all of Mom and Dad's attention. No longer could I sing and shout whenever I wanted, because "the baby was sleeping." No longer did Mom spend all her time playing with me; no, "little brother" needed all her attention. I was left feeling abandoned and powerless. Powerless to command my parents' attention. Powerless to get my way in kindergarten when I wanted a particular toy, but someone else was already playing with it. Powerless to stay in bed as long as I wanted or to stay up as late at night as I wanted. By the time I reached that first-grade classroom, I had spent several years—an eternity for a six-year-old—feeling bewildered and angry about that loss of power.

Now, all that was about to end. I was to be let into the real secrets of magic and take back all that power I had lost. Oh, I was ready! Holding my breath, I turned the page, ready for all that awaited me.

You can imagine my utter disappointment when what greeted me was not some deep secret of universal power, but a trick—a silly way to make a knot seem to appear in a handkerchief. It was an explanation of how to fool people into believing I could make some useless knot appear in some useless handkerchief, as if by magic—instructions for perpetuating a fraud! Instead of magic, the book was teaching me to deceive others.

To say I was upset would put it too mildly. This charlatan writer had perpetrated an outrage on me!

Nevertheless, I had the book, and I was committed to doing a book report on it, so I had to read it. As I did so, I amused myself by learning some of the tricks. Maybe it would be fun to fool people into believing I had magic powers, even though I most definitely did not. When I presented the book report in class, I performed one of the tricks; I believe it was done with a Life Saver candy on a piece of string, showing how I could take the Life Saver off the string while someone else held both ends, then put it back. I gave the book a lukewarm review: "It's just a bunch of silly tricks, but it's kind of interesting learning how they're done." I don't remember what response the trick got, but I do remember the anxiety of presenting it, praying that nothing would go wrong and that I wouldn't accidentally reveal the secret.

That is my first memory of magic—disappointment that it did not yield the power I expected but fascination with the secrets I did discover there. This experience was the first layer of revelation in what was to become a lifelong unveiling.

Secret Knowledge

I suppose it was that first book on magic that gave me a taste for secret knowledge. Later, I became fascinated by science, realizing that it, too, revealed secrets—and provided other benefits as well.

I distinctly remember a moment of life-changing impact: in third or fourth grade, as I was enthusiastically telling a friend about the wonders of Scarabaeoidea—aka the dung beetle (I was, after all, a nine-year-old boy)—a girl sitting at a desk in the next aisle turned and said, "Wow. You're really smart!" At that moment, for the first time, I began to think of myself as an intelligent person.

Of course, it wasn't until much later that I realized how lucky I was that she hadn't turned and said, "Ugh . . . you boys are so stupid; all you can think about is a bunch of disgusting bugs!" I am quite sure that at that impressionable age, being called a stupid person would have defined a role for me just as strongly as being called a smart person, a gift unwittingly bestowed.

Throughout my life, I have continued to be fascinated by secret or hidden information. I was an unusual child who actually loved learning and somehow understood what a luxury it was to have a time in my life that could be dedicated completely to that. My school years were happy in many ways, but I was never quite satisfied with knowing only what everyone else did. I wanted to understand the secrets, the so-called forbidden knowledge, and I wanted to know why it should be forbidden. What were they keeping from us, anyway?

I have come to think that this thirst for hidden knowledge is one of the primary things that set wizards apart from most other people.

Wizards love learning the secrets of how the world works. They want to know the secrets of persuasion or secret ways of doing things that look "just like magic." They want to know all about the secret powers incorporated in people, organizations, and nature. Sometimes they just like knowing things that other people don't. Knowing all those secrets makes it possible for a wizard to do things others believe to be impossible.

This book is at least partly about revealing some of the true wizard's secrets that I've discovered—and also some magicians' secrets. You will read about techniques for contacting your subconscious mind—rewriting your own stories, accessing trance states, and others—but also about how we create illusions by combining the mind's unstoppable ability to recognize patterns (even when there are none!) with the ability to direct attention.

Many of the "secrets" I will reveal aren't really secret at all. They are, as folks say, "hidden in plain sight." Some "secrets" are things most of us have chosen not to know because we think it would be inappropriate or painful for us to know them. Society builds taboos around much of this knowledge—things that are not immoral or illegal but are nevertheless things "nice people" would never do.

I remember, for example, when I was much younger and more naïve than I am now, being taken aback when I discovered the difference between wholesale and retail prices. How dare stores I had trusted take such large markups? It didn't seem fair that I should have to pay $12 for a shirt that the store had only paid $3 for. What a rip-off! That this was something I had not considered or chosen to know about until I was in my late teens or early twenties still amazes me a bit. For me, then, discovering how businesses operate was learning "secret knowledge." Perhaps I was a bit dense, but I suspect there are many people who have never given a second thought to where products come from, how they make their way to stores, or why they cost what they do. This is the arcane knowledge of the wizards of retail.

Performers' Secrets

As a teenager, I became interested in acting and in directing plays. I think it was my way of finding a secondary family in which I was automatically accepted and praised for my talent and intelligence. It was especially important to me during my teen years, when I, like most teenagers, was wondering whether I would ever really fit in and be accepted by my peers.

I quickly became passionate about acting and all aspects of the theater, and decided I wanted to make a life in the theater. As an actor, one could magically transform oneself and reproduce experiences and emotions that would otherwise be unacceptable—or at least mildly frightening. While we might enjoy seeing the trials and tribulations of Othello or Macbeth—or Dirty Harry—at a safe distance as they play out on a stage or screen, we certainly wouldn't want those events playing out for real in our living room or classroom.

Later, I discovered I was missing some of the pieces one needed to build a successful career as an actor. As a twenty-year-old, revealing my innermost emotions wasn't something I was prepared to do, so I decided to pursue a career as a director and producer instead. My models at the time were Broadway director/producer Harold Prince and Gordon Craig, who advocated a particular kind of "total theater" in which the director's and designer's jobs were combined and elevated to create a new kind of "artist of the theater."

> *You will remember that at the commencement of our conversation I told you my belief in the Renaissance of the Art of the Theater was based in my belief in the Renaissance of the stage-director, and that when he had understood the right use of actors, scene, costume, lighting, and dance, and by means of these had mastered the crafts of interpretation, he would then gradually acquire the mastery of action, line, color, rhythm, and words, this last strength developing out of all the rest. . . . Then I said the Art of the Theater would have won back its rights, and its work would stand self-reliant as a creative art, and no longer as an interpretive craft.*
>
> —Gordon Craig, "The Artist of the Theater,"
> from *Directors on Directing* [2]

My years of training to be a director were what added most to my arsenal of wizard's skills. A director's specialty is creating and molding effective experiences for audiences. A director uses both obvious and subtle means to create a specific theatrical experience. As we shall see, wizards create and manage change for themselves and the world around them by designing and creating just such transformative experiences, using many of the same techniques.

As a stage director, one learns the importance of action, character, setting, rhythm, lighting, music, and many other elements in the creation of an experience. One learns how profoundly a particular experience can be affected by things occurring beneath the level of a person's consciousness. Have you ever watched a particularly dramatic movie with the sound turned off? Try it next time you play a rented movie. Choose a particularly dramatic scene and watch it both with and without the soundtrack. If you have never done this, you will be amazed at what a huge contribution a good soundtrack makes to the emotional effect of a film. Yet when we watch a film, we are seldom consciously aware of the background music and sounds. Music is only one of the ways we can shade the experiences we create for ourselves and others. Setting, lighting, ambiance, previous experiences—all have a much larger influence on all of our experiences than we generally realize.

Life with Magicians

After I completed my master's degree in directing and design for the theater, I spent several years teaching various subjects in the performing arts and then quite a few more years working in New York, managing Broadway and off-Broadway theater as well as some small dance companies. Like so many young people, I discovered that the thing I had dreamed of doing was, in the real world, not quite what I had imagined it to be. I moved to working almost exclusively with performing magicians—directing, advising, and helping them create their shows. I loved working with these performers, who use their magic to open up hearts and minds to the possibility that there are, as Hamlet put it, "more things in heaven and earth, Horatio, than are dreamt of in your philosophy."[3]

Through my work, particularly with Jeff McBride, Eugene Burger, and Robert E. Neale (some of whom you'll be hearing more about a bit later), I found myself inquiring into the deeper nature of that thing we all called "magic" and its relationship to both my personal experience and that of the society around me. We created a special event, The Mystery School, a three-day annual retreat at which we gathered a group of magicians and explored subjects such as why we did magic, what it was for, what it meant to claim the title "magician," and so on. We tried to figure out exactly what we meant by the words *magic* and *magical experience* and tried to find ways of giving one another just that sort of experience.

It has been over 20 years since that first Mystery School, and I have been exploring magic ever since. I have had many discussions and given long thought to just what magic is and what it is for. I have learned much about the techniques that stage magicians and others use to create magical experiences for their audiences. I have learned how to create deceptions and illusions and how to give those things meaning. Beyond that, I have taken on the same quest that my friends did—a quest to find real magic—whatever that means.

Several years ago, it occurred to me that this knowledge—the secrets behind magicians' tricks; the secrets learned from "real" magicians such as shamans, yogis, and others; and the secrets known to all successful per-formers—could be useful for everyone, just as my mother had told me way back when we read Stanislavsky's book on acting together.

At that point, I came to the conclusion that by sharing this informa-tion, I would be providing the means to create real-life wizards. Having read enthusiastically about wizards from the time I was very young and having spent so much of my life with people I had come to think of as wiz-ards, I thought I knew more than enough about the subject to write this book. I was mistaken, rapidly discovering that almost every line I wrote raised questions for which I lacked clear answers. Instead of sitting down to write a book, I had assigned myself the job of re-educating myself on the subject of wizardry.

Now, over three years later, I find that my ideas have coalesced into something more meaningful, although they continue to shift and grow. I have had long, sometimes heated, and always informative discussions with some fascinating people and read extensively about many others whom I think of as real-life wizards. You will meet many of them in the next chapter.

Along the way, I have discovered principles I never knew existed. Patterns were pointed out to me that, although they are right there in plain sight, are seldom noticed by anyone who's not a wizard. Real wizards taught me techniques for taking control of my own mind and for influencing the minds of those around me. I have heard dozens of amazing stories and been both inspired and humbled by what I have found.

After all that, I am convinced more than ever that the secrets of actors, singers, performing magicians, hypnotists, and many others are just the sort of secrets a real wizard loves—and needs. You will find a great many of those secrets laid out for you in the pages that follow, with suggestions on how you can learn to use them yourself.

I know my own quest to learn more of the wizard's ways will continue. I hope that the rest of this book will not only amaze and entertain you but also inspire you in your own quest to become a real wizard. The pace of change in our world continues to accelerate at a dizzying rate, and we need more wise, responsible, and powerful wizards every day. Please join me now on the journey!

Notes

1. White, T.H. *The Once and Future King*, page 287.
2. Cole, Toby & Krich Chinoy, Helen. *Directors on Directing*, page 161.
3. Shakespeare, William. *Hamlet*, Act 1, scene 6.

A Wizard Is...

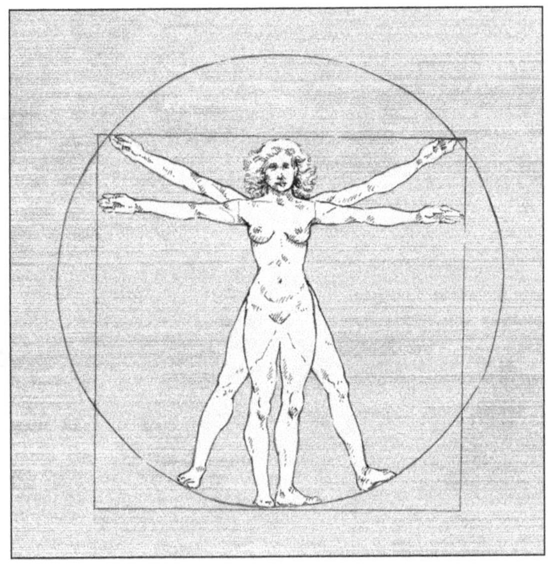

A Wizard Is...

NOUN

*1 A man who has magical powers, especially in legends
and fairy tales.*

*1.1 A person who is very skilled in a particular field or
activity.*

Origin

*late Middle English (in the sense 'philosopher, sage'):
from wise1 + -ard.*

— Oxford English Dictionary, American Version

After several years of questioning myself, reading many books, and talking with pretty much any of my friends and acquaintances who I thought might know something about the subject, I have discovered that a wizard is not just someone who does magic or someone who does magic outside of magic shows. A wizard is not just someone who uses the techniques of magic in real life, although that is certainly one of the things a wizard does.

I asked about a thousand people (Facebook friends), "If you had Merlyn's powers, what would you do?" I got hundreds of answers. The clearest and most consistent one was in the negative: "I wouldn't be doing magic shows, that's for sure." Things like "I'd save the environment" and "I'd put an end to poverty" were way up there, and not a few folks would have gone right to Las Vegas and won a gazillion dollars at the tables.

Ultimately, the best and most useful answers came from my closest wizard friends, Jeff and Abbi McBride, Eugene Burger, and Lawrence Hass, all members of the faculty of Jeff McBride's Magic & Mystery School. Each started their definition with the obvious: A wizard is a wise person. You can tell by the word itself: a "Wise-ard" is one who has wisdom.

I later concluded, largely through discussions with corporate wizard George Parker, that wizards are all about change. Their job is to facilitate change in themselves and others. As human beings, we often find change to be difficult. We like the comfort of the ruts we carve for ourselves, even if those ruts lead to stagnation and suffering. Those who seem to be too ready for change often make us a bit uncomfortable; but without them, society would stagnate, as it did during the Middle Ages, which are also called the "Dark Ages" because during that period, change was stifled and society stagnated.

These two things together, then: Wisdom combined with higher-than-average ability to facilitate change, seem to me to be the primary criteria for defining someone as a wizard. This may seem simple, and in many ways, it is. However, it is not easy to achieve.

Why You Want to Become a Wizard

What will you gain by becoming a wizard? The answer really boils down to this: Wizards take control of their own lives, developing their own abilities and actively seeking out the wisdom they need in order to better connect with and affect the world around them. If you want to live a life with meaning and purpose and have a positive effect on the world, your best path is that of the wizard.

In legend and in history, great wizards seem to appear at turning points—times of great change. This pattern occurs because the wizard's role is essentially that of change agent. Wizards often both instigate and smooth the way for great changes. In our time, the rate of change has accelerated almost beyond what anyone 50 years ago might have imagined possible. As a result, the world needs more wizards now than at any other time in our history.

Most people in our society tend to go along with the herd, almost without thinking. We are born, educated (trained), go to work, get married, raise a family, retire, and die, all while living in a kind of group trance, running the programs society dictates for us, without ever really questioning those programs or choosing a particular life or path. We might affect a few lives as we go, making our spouses and our children either happy or crazy or affecting a few co-workers. But when most of us are confronted with real change—the kind that does away with a conventional job and a conventional employer-employee relationship almost overnight or moves us from one economic or political paradigm to another—we have no idea what to do or how to cope. We have not been taught how to think or to fend for ourselves in any way outside our norms.

A wizard, on the other hand, questions everything, all the time. A wizard is less concerned with ideas of not fitting in or of being cast out of a group for her strange ways or beliefs. She has come to those beliefs through observation of nature and firsthand experience of the world around her, and she has done her own thinking. She is quite sure of what she thinks and feels, even as she leaves open the possibility that her thoughts and feelings might be subject to change when she is confronted with additional information.

This constant questioning, this willingness to become a real agent of change, gives a confidence and sense of power most people lack. In these times of rapid and often disruptive change, the wizard's way is a way to create a meaningful life and to positively affect the world we all live in.

And That's What a Wizard Is!

We've seen, then, that a wizard is someone who has amassed wisdom through experience. Wizards learn to think for themselves and to question everything. They are agents of change, unafraid to explore and think differently.

Before I go too deeply into specific techniques, ideas, or the wizard's way, allow me to introduce you to some of the people I consider to be true wizards. These are my models—the people I have been talking to or studying to discover what sets them apart. From them, I have received my own education in regard to wizards, and I think it is only fair that I introduce them so you can get to know each one just a bit before I start revealing their secrets to you.

Wizard's Work

Before looking at the following chapter, make a list of people who have lived or are living the life of a true wizard as we've defined it here. Think of at least five such people, and write a sentence or two for each one, explaining what it is about them that you think qualifies them as a real wizard.

Chapter 2

A Gallery of Wizards

A Gallery of Wizards

Here's to the crazy ones. The misfits. The rebels. The troublemakers. The round pegs in the square holes.

The ones who see things differently. They're not fond of rules. And they have no respect for the status quo. You can quote them, disagree with them, glorify or vilify them.

But the only thing you can't do is ignore them. Because they change things. They invent. They imagine. They heal. They explore. They create. They inspire. They push the human race forward.

—Rob Siltanen with participation of Lee Clow[1]

To assist us in understanding what it really means to be a wizard, let's examine the stories of wizards from fiction and from history, from the past and from the present. In this chapter, we will look at wizards of legend and story: Merlyn, Gandalf, the wizards of the Harry Potter stories, and the Wizard of Oz. We will also learn about some real-life wizards. Leonardo da Vinci, Mohandas Gandhi, Steve Jobs, and Albert Einstein may be the best known; however, some less well known but powerful contemporary wizards like George Parker, Sylvia Brallier, Oberon Zell-Ravenheart, and Jeff McBride may have even more to teach us than their more famous counterparts. By examining their stories, we may begin to get a clear picture of what they all have in common—the characteristics that make each one a wizard—as well as the specific traits that make him or her a particular kind of wizard.

Merlyn

"The best thing for being sad," replied Merlyn,
beginning to puff and blow, "is to learn something. That's
the only thing that never fails."

— T. H. White, The Once and Future King[2]

When I hear the word wizard, an image of Merlyn flashes into my mind. I'm sure you know this image. He has a long white beard and hair; he wears a high, pointed hat and long robes, perhaps adorned with stars and moons; and he commands vast unseen forces. He is wise and powerful, mysterious, and on the side of good.

Not too many years after encountering *The First Book of Magic*, I was introduced to Merlyn when my parents gave me a copy of *King Arthur and His Knights*.[3] Merlyn is a somewhat shadowy presence in that particular telling of the myth. Although he is "accused of being a witch" and performs several feats of magic, he is primarily an advisor to King Arthur and is seen mostly as a background character.

It was not until a few years later, when I read T. H. White's fantastic novel *The Once and Future King* and the follow-up *The Book of Merlyn*[3], that this prototypical wizard really came alive in my imagination. Who was this strange being, this wise and powerful man who slid mysteriously in and out of the narrative, educating the young Arthur, appearing at opportune moments to assist him, and then fading out of sight again? Where did he come from, and how did he get those wizardly powers? Often in disguise, often off in other parts of the kingdom influencing who knows what, Merlyn seemed a mage of great power and mystery. Obviously in possession of not only occult knowledge and magical powers but also the wisdom to make use of them effectively, Merlyn affected history itself.

Inspired, I began to read every new re-telling of the tale of Merlyn and Arthur I could get my hands on. To this day, I am excited when I discover that a new author has taken on the task of re-telling the tale, each from a slightly different perspective, adding his or her own new insights. As I read more and grew into young manhood, I found Arthur and his knights slowly paling in my imagination into rather dull, almost interchangeable warrior characters with little depth, but my fascination with Merlyn, the myth of Avalon, and the magic of the British Isles and the Celtic people grew and grew.

The Merlyn who lives in my imagination today is not drawn from any one particular telling of the tale but combines bits and pieces from all of them. I see him as a real flesh-and-blood human being, probably related to Arthur. I imagine that early in life, he fell in with some of the local wise women. Perhaps his noble mother died when he was a baby and he was taken in by one or more of the fascinating women who lived at the edges of small towns or villages somewhere in Cornwall or Wales and served as midwives and healers. Living at the edge of the forest, they knew the lore of wild herbs and the ways of the small creatures of the wood. Perhaps they knew how to make a few simple charms as well, to ward off evil or attract a lover.

As a boy, Merlyn would have learned all that he could from these women and would have become familiar with all aspects of village life, possibly as something of an outsider because of his association with the witch women. Being an exceptionally quick and bright boy, though, he would have come to the attention of a local Druid. The Druids were a priestly class, keepers of secret knowledge at a time when Great Britain had been ruled for some time by Romans, who had brought Christianity with them and were spreading it through the British Isles. As the Roman Empire pulled back, though, the older religions of the Celtic tribes would have seen a resurgence. Young Merlyn would have been a lover of secrets, and his sharp mind would have snapped up knowledge from every tradition he encountered, both the older Celtic traditions and the new Roman ones. He would have been able to draw from, evaluate, and synthesize that knowledge for himself, free from the dogma of any one tradition.

As a young man in the last years of Roman rule, probably from a lesser noble family, Merlyn would have learned to be a warrior. Many versions of his story tell of his feats on the battlefield as well as his magical accomplishments. He would also have been a bard—a keeper of historical lore in the form of songs.

What are the particular traits of this individual, this magical Merlyn, that distinguish him as a wizard? What are his relevant characteristics?

Merlyn appears to have been a visionary, one of the few who envisioned a Great Britain whose people, both those of the old religion and those more influenced by (and often part of) the Roman occupation and the Christian influence that came with it, would come to see themselves as a single people, a nation. Merlyn was not only able to hold this vision but apparently took on a personal quest to make it a reality. It was he who arranged for Igraine, Arthur's mother, who came from the Celtic tribes, more steeped in the old religion and ways, and Uther, his Roman father, to come together to create Arthur. It was Merlyn who saw to Arthur's unorthodox education and Merlyn's magic that ultimately revealed him to be the rightful heir to the throne.

Another of Merlyn's prime wizardly attributes was undoubtedly his possession of secret knowledge. He is portrayed as a wise and learned man at a time when learned men were rare. Something of a recluse, he spent long hours studying exotic flora and fauna. He was able to read signs in the heavens and undertake tasks that seemed impossible to his less educated contemporaries.

For me, one of Merlyn's more interesting traits is that he often operated behind the scenes. He was never the ruler himself, but through his efforts, the king was able to rule. There appear to have been long periods when Merlyn was not at court but was busy in his crystal cave or traveling in disguise. At other times, he appeared at court, helping to structure and direct the king's affairs. He was often an outsider, able to stand aside and observe what was going on at court and in the kingdom from an outsider's perspective. At the same time, through his relationship with the king, he could step inside the court and into the spotlight, taking over and directing the affairs of the king and his kingdom as an ultimate insider.

Dumbledore and the Harry Potter Universe

"It does not do to dwell on dreams and forget to live, remember that."

— Albus Dumbledore[4]

J. K. Rowling's fantastically imagined universe of the Harry Potter books is a unique world of wizards in which nearly everyone is supposed to be a wizard or a witch, the wizard's female counterpart. Those who are not wizards, called "Muggles," are mostly unaware of the whole world of wizardry. Yet even in the wizards' world, where all people have varying degrees of magical power, not everyone is a true wizard, at least by my definition. Many are simply sorcerers, soothsayers, or tricksters who have not yet developed the wisdom and commitment to be true wizards.

Of course, Albus Dumbledore stands out as one of the true wizards. He has many of the attributes of a wizard that I listed in connection with Merlyn: He loves learning. He has had a great many experiences of life, from which he has learned true wisdom. Perhaps most importantly, he influences the course of events in his world, orchestrating the battle against Voldemort and his minions. A great deal of his work is behind the scenes, molding the young students in his care not only through classes but by guiding them into the sort of real-world experiences and adventures most of our modern schools would never allow.

Dumbledore also seems to have the knack of seeing the world around him as a four-dimensional web and knowing just how to pluck at the strands of that web in order to achieve results larger than would seem possible from such small actions. He lets Harry in on particular secrets but not others and guides him into his various adventures. He sees to it that Hermione has the time turner and learns to use it, just in time for her to use it to save the day. The Harry Potter books detail many small incidents in which Dumbledore influences the outcome of events by exerting a small influence on one or more of the players in the forefront of the action, providing them with just enough of an advantage to swing the outcome.

Although I wouldn't say that all the wizards in the Harry Potter stories qualify as real wizards, the overall story is about how Harry and his close friends become real wizards. Their school learning in magic gives them a sorcerer's powers, but it is their experiences—the battles and ordeals—that provide them with the wisdom they need in order to grow into the powerful wizards they ultimately become.

Gandalf

With Dwarf and Hobbit, Elves and Men,

with mortal and immortal folk,

with bird on bough and beast in den,

in their own secret tongues he spoke.

A deadly sword, a healing hand,

a back that bent beneath its load;

a trumpet-voice, a burning brand,

a weary pilgrim on the road.

A lord of wisdom throned he sat,

swift in anger, quick to laugh;

an old man in a battered hat,

who leaned upon a thorny staff.

—Frodo's song for Gandalf from *The Fellowship of the Ring* by J.R.R. Tolkien[5]

The wizard Gandalf leads the fight against the evil wizard Sauron in J.R.R. Tolkien's trilogy *The Lord of the Rings* and his story *The Hobbit*. Gandalf, a wizard learned in the ways of the many peoples who inhabit Middle-earth, orchestrates many of the happenings that ultimately come together to defeat Sauron. Gandalf is the mysterious stranger who moves from one part of Middle-earth to another, leading the reader from one part of the story to another.

Like many of the wizards of legend, Gandalf's powers are not only those of the magician or sorcerer, although he certainly has such powers. He is the link between the many peoples of Middle-earth, and he uses his knowledge of all of them, along with his unique vision and his persuasive abilities, to bring them all into the ultimate battle against evil. Although Gandalf does use his magical powers during the story, it is his wisdom and his ability to see the connections between the various peoples who make up Middle-earth, combined with the courage to take full responsibility for what is happening that make the difference in vanquishing Sauron.

Wizard of Oz

> *"Then suddenly the wind changed, and the balloon floated down into the heart of this noble city, where I was instantly acclaimed Oz, the First Wizard de Luxe!*
>
> *"Times being what they were, I accepted the job, retaining my balloon against the advent of a quick get-away."*

—The Wizard, in The Wizard of Oz, screenplay by Noel Langley, Florence Ryerson, and Edgar Allen Woolf, after the book by L. Frank Baum[6]

In the classic movie *The Wizard of Oz*, we have a slightly different sort of wizard: the Wizard starts out as a bit of an imposter, yet he is able to grant all of the main characters' wishes simply by helping each of them shift their point of view.

The Wizard begins as a carnival magician, con artist, and balloonist, a charlatan and an outsider in his own world before finding himself accidentally transported to the land of Oz. Landing in this magical world courtesy of a hot air balloon, he is immediately hailed by the people of Oz as a great wizard. He is happy to accept the role. He creates a complicated machine to work all the special effects that will make him seem to be a wizard and then hides within the machine in order to interact with his subjects.

Like Merlyn, Gandalf, and the others, this wizard has a nemesis—the Wicked Witch of the West. He sends Dorothy and her party off to vanquish the witch on his behalf, never expecting them to return alive. When they do, he is exposed as the charlatan he believes himself to be. However, through the clever use of some commonplace wisdom, he finds he is able to give the Scarecrow, the Tin Man, and the Cowardly Lion just the things they need in order to become whole.

It is interesting that in the story of Oz, the wizard himself feels he has no magical powers. On one level, it is the story of a common person who has been thrust into a role far greater than he knows himself to be. When he stops hiding behind his curtain, though, he steps into that role of wizard and actually becomes one. When forced to take on the responsibility that comes with the role, he finds he has what it takes. He discovers that he does have the necessary wisdom to set things right and actually becomes the wizard he has been pretending to be!

Leonardo da Vinci

> *The acquisition of any knowledge whatever is always useful to the intellect, because it will be able to banish the useless things and retain those which are good. For nothing can be either loved or hated unless it is first known.*
>
> —Leonardo da Vinci, from Leonardo's Notebooks[7]

Given his position as the illegitimate son of a village lawyer, Leonardo da Vinci's prospects in life seemed less than promising.

As a schoolboy, I was introduced to Leonardo primarily as an artist, known for the relatively few of his paintings that have come down to us. His Mona Lisa and The Last Supper are probably the best known. He is also known as one of the greatest examples of a Renaissance man, someone who is well versed in many fields. Leonardo as the archetypal Renaissance man is especially interesting because da Vinci lacked any kind of formal education. For a time, he was allowed to serve as an apprentice at the studio of Andrea del Verrocchio, where he encountered many formally educated upper-class young men. An encounter with one of them prompted him to write in one of his many notebooks,

"I am fully aware that the fact of my not being a man of letters may cause certain arrogant persons to think that they may with reason censure me, alleging that I am a man ignorant of book-learning. Foolish folk! Do they not know that I might retort by saying, as did Marius to the Roman Patricians: 'They who themselves go about adorned in the labour of others will not permit me my own'? They will say that because of my lack of book-learning, I cannot properly express what I desire to treat of. Do they not know that my subjects require for their exposition experience rather than the words of others?"[7]

Although we know him primarily for his paintings, Leonardo in fact made his living mostly by other means. For a time, he was an advisor to the infamous Cesare Borgia, designing the war machines and many strategies that helped Borgia conquer a large part of northern Italy. For another part of his career, Leonardo designed and organized extravagant parties and ceremonies for the Duke of Milan.

Da Vinci is an important example of a wizard for a number of reasons. Not the least is his insistence on learning directly from nature and through his own experience and thought rather than accepting blindly the knowledge written in books. Through this process, da Vinci made a number of scientific discoveries, which were written up in his notebooks and which were often claimed by others in much later periods. His notebooks are filled with detailed drawings of inventions never realized in his own time that anticipated airplanes, helicopters, and other machines. Da Vinci's real-life experience also informed his writings on art. Some of his writings about the art of painting could be dropped directly into a modern textbook for directors of either theater or film with no hint of being out of date.

Another of da Vinci's wizardly qualities was his ability to use an outsider's point of view to better understand things he wished to study. For example, he applied his knowledge of engineering to create new ways of casting large sculpture. His skills as a painter were his key to better understanding and recording his discoveries in botany, anatomy, and zoology. And da Vinci's knowledge of mechanics made it possible for him to create the spectacles he produced for his wealthy patrons.

It is easy to forget that during da Vinci's life, his native Florence and all of northern Italy were constantly at war. He and his friend Niccolo Machiavelli acted much as Merlyn was reputed to have done, forging alliances and shaping the society around them through indirect means. While serving those who were in power, da Vinci and Machiavelli used their experience and influence to make small changes that would drastically influence the direction of the major political and social change going on around them.

Leonardo lived to question everything, insisting on learning through direct observation and the operation of his own mind rather than relying on the thoughts of others set down in books. He was unafraid to think and experiment outside of the particular field he was working in, a trait which fed his phenomenal ability to develop scientific understanding through his artwork and to invent machines and weapons far ahead of his time by applying knowledge he had acquired through studying anatomy and biology. His embodiment of the Renaissance ideal of developing facility in many different areas, his willingness to operate creatively to make things happen, and his refusal to see any project as impossible make him a quintessential example of what it means to be a true wizard.

Albert Einstein

"Unthinking respect for authority is the greatest enemy of truth."

Albert Einstein[8]

Albert Einstein is among my favorite real-life wizard characters. Not only do his halo of unruly white hair and bushy mustache give him the look of a real wizard, but his accomplishments and way of approaching life and work are great examples of the way a real wizard functions.

Einstein is reputed to have been a poor student when he was young, but at least one biographer refutes those stories. As a youngster, Einstein seems to have been extremely bright but a decided renegade who insisted on thinking freely and questioning everything. Professors of his time believed that their students ought to conform and show respect for existing knowledge. As a result, at the age of 24, instead of having his doctorate and a professorship at a major university (as many of his friends and colleagues with lesser intellect and worse grades already did), Einstein found himself a clerk in the Swiss patent office.

During his stint at the patent office, Einstein wrote the four papers that would change the way we understand our physical world for all time. He made each discovery by examining principles that were widely accepted but encompassed conflicting elements, trying to figure how they could be reconciled. Through a series of thought experiments, Einstein was able to find just where the underlying assumptions behind each of the principles failed and then create a new perspective that resolved the conflicts. In doing so, he established the basis of quantum mechanics, proposed a new theory of electrodynamics, and created his famous theory of special relativity. He also presented a new way of explaining Brownian motion that established the reality of atoms for the first time. He did all this in his spare time during that one year, without ever setting foot in a laboratory!

Many wizards—Einstein, Feynman, da Vinci and others—prefer to discover or re-discover basic laws of nature through direct observation and through their own reasoning, exhibiting a marked unwillingness to accept something as true just because someone else has said or written it.

For me, the traits that make Einstein a wizard are his willingness to think and work outside the mainstream of thought and his insatiable curiosity. "Question everything," Einstein's lifelong motto, would make a great watchword for any would-be wizard.

Mary Ellen Pleasant

"No more independent woman ever wore shoe leather."

San Francisco Chronicle , writing about
Mary Ellen Pleasant, 1895

It is difficult to find female wizards in history. I believe this is largely because Western culture made it necessary for women who were true wizards to hide their power, often working through men who got much of the credit for the work the women did. We do, however, know the stories of a few female wizards—for example, the story of Mary Ellen Pleasant. Known as "Mammy Pleasant" and "The Voodoo Queen of San Francisco," this woman managed to amass a huge fortune and to influence the actions of the rich and powerful throughout northern California for much of the second half of the nineteenth century.

Mary Ellen Pleasant was able to achieve so much by using the kind of secret knowledge and abilities available only to those who truly understand the wizard's way. Her wide range of experiences early in life gave her a unique perspective on the web of commerce, class, and society that was the San Francisco of her time. This secret knowledge gave her influence over both the rich and powerful and those who served them. Her story, which we will explore in the chapters on working the web and role-playing, provides wonderful examples of how wizards can use their secret knowledge and abilities to take control of their own life and the world around them.

Mohandas Gandhi

"We must become the change we want to see in the world."

—Mahatma Gandhi[9]

Mohandas Gandhi is a wonderful example of a real-life wizard. As a skinny old man dressed in a loincloth, he brought about the overthrow of the

British Raj in India by refusing to eat. Now, that's leverage!

Gandhi's fiercely principled battle for human dignity and against injustice and bigotry, first in South Africa and later in India, is a powerful illustration of how much one man, without either personal wealth or the usual accoutrements of power, can achieve. Along the way, Gandhi transformed himself profoundly, from a somewhat dandified young lawyer seeking traditional success with all its upper middle-class trappings to a man without material possessions who spent his days spinning yarn, who nonetheless transformed India.

Like many real-life wizards, Gandhi was able to remove himself from the mainstream and its unquestioned assumptions. Through an unwavering dedication to principles he thought out largely for himself, Gandhi was able to completely transform both himself and the subcontinent of India. Later, Gandhi's principles of *satyagraha*—resistance to injustice through mass civil disobedience—and *ahimsa*—dedication to nonviolent means—inspired the civil rights and the anti-war movements in the United States in the 1950s and 1960s and the anti-apartheid movement spearheaded by Nelson Mandela in South Africa. Thus, Gandhi is a wizard who continued to change the world long after his death.

Oberon Zell-Ravenheart

> *The best way to predict the future is to create it. . . .*
> *The wizard has the power to create the future he wants.*
> *To manifest what you desire will enable you to predict the*
> *future.*
>
> —Oberon Zell-Ravenheart,
> **Grimoire for the Apprentice Wizard**[10]

Oberon Zell-Ravenheart runs a modern school for wizards called the "Grey School of Wizardry." If you see him at a public event, he might be arrayed in full wizard regalia: dark robe, tall pointed hat, and staff topped with a large crystal. Oberon inhabits the role of a wizard as fully as anyone I know. Although Oberon's idea of what it takes to be a wizard in our world differs somewhat from mine, we can learn a great deal from him.

Early in life, Oberon became one of the first leaders of the neo-pagan movement in America—a movement that by some accounts has grown to over 1 million adherents world wide and has been reported to be the fastest-growing religion in the United States (based on percentage growth), its numbers more than doubling in the past 10 years. His willingness to think and act outside the mainstream has led him to create an extremely interesting and unusual life and to inspire thousands of others to do the same. He teaches us the value of renegade thinking and of using a creative, active mind-set to do the "impossible."

Steve Jobs

Your time is limited, so don't waste it living someone else's life. Don't be trapped by dogma— which is living with the results of other people's thinking.

—Steve Jobs, commencement address
at Stanford University, 2005[11]

Steve Jobs might be the best known of my contemporary wizards. Well known as the leader of the incredibly successful companies Apple and Pixar, he has been widely acknowledged as a brilliant business leader. It's the way his brilliance worked, however, that makes him, in my mind, a true wizard. Let's have a quick look at some of the highlights of his career to see why.

After dropping out of college, Jobs, with his partner Steve Wozniak, created one of the first personal computers and started Apple Computer (now Apple Inc.). There was virtually no personal computer industry at the time. Like many of Jobs's later achievements, his first product fulfilled a need and created a market for a product that almost no one knew they wanted at the time. Throughout his career, Jobs's unique personal vision gave him the ability to take existing technologies and combine them in new ways, improve their usability, or make other improvements that others had not yet imagined. In doing so, he created whole new markets for the products his company built. An early example of Jobs's vision is his introduction of the graphical user interface in Apple's Lisa computer and the first Macintosh, which revolutionized the publishing industry and made the personal computer a tool accessible to everyone, not just the geeks.

One clue to Jobs's approach to business and to life comes from a popular story about how Jobs lured John Sculley away from PepsiCo to serve as Apple's CEO in 1983. His hook? "Do you want to sell sugar water for the rest of your life, or do you want to come with me and change the world?" Jobs was never content to just go along with someone else's program. From the beginning, nothing less than changing the world would do for Steve Jobs.

Jobs purchased Lucasfilm's Computer Graphics Division (later christened Pixar), and from 1986 until it was sold to the Walt Disney Company in 2006, he helped it turn out one mega-hit after another. To this day, Pixar remains the only major studio never to produce a flop. It has achieved this record by using a carefully crafted creative and production process that re-invented the way films—especially animated films—are made. At a time when the animated feature was thought to be a dying art form, Jobs saw opportunities to re-invent the whole process and implemented his vision, resulting in remarkable success. After his return to Apple in 1996, Jobs transformed that company, which had become sluggish and lacking in vision while he was away, into the world leader in the consumer electronics industry. First with the iMac, then the iPod & iTunes, the iPhone, and, more recently, the iPad, he re-thought and re-created one segment of the consumer tech industry after another, branding both the products and the industries with the Apple logo. Each product was created as a result of Jobs's ability to see the tech world and various markets from a perspective that no one else seemed to share, along with an unflinching commitment to his own vision of excellence.

Since Jobs' return, one thing that sets Apple's products apart from all others is attention to designing users' experience with a product. Every moment, from the first thing a user feels when they pick up the product to the way a screen comes to life when the power is turned on, has been considered, and the experience of each moment has been consciously designed. Jobs and his company are not only visionaries but also the conscious designers of experiences for everyone who comes into contact with one of their products. Rather than playing catch-up and trying to build small, incremental changes into a product that a competitor has had success with, Apple consistently designs its products from the ground up, with unparalleled attention to design, user experience, and quality.

From the beginning, Jobs saw technology primarily as a means of empowering creativity. First in publishing, then graphics, then music, he was never a technologist for technology's sake, a mind-set that made him a renegade thinker in the high-tech world of Silicon Valley.

Jeff McBride

I have had the opportunity for radical reinvention a few times in my life—and I look forward to more!

—Jeff McBride, *The Museletter*, March 2014[12]

Jeff McBride has been my client and one of my closest friends for well over twenty years now. He is a true magician's magician and a real wizard who has profoundly influenced the course of performance magic in our time. He is included here, however, not because of his work as one of the top magical performers in the world but because I've been privileged to see him, time and time again, remake himself. He continues to show the courage and the willingness to seek and learn from new experiences, to let go of parts of himself that may not serve, and to use new experience and knowledge to transform himself.

When I first met Jeff, he had already been a Las Vegas headliner and opening act for such superstars as Diana Ross and Tom Jones. At the age of 25, he had already seen most of his boyhood dreams come true but was surprised to find himself deeply dissatisfied. A friend at the time told him, "It's because you want the magic to be real—to be a real magician—and you know you're a fake."

At about the same time, Bill Moyers was interviewing Joseph Campbell in his series *The Power of Myth* on PBS, and both Jeff and I found the series to be inspiring. Magic had been a significant part of civilization for several millennia; only recently had it been packaged as light entertainment. We set ourselves the goal of creating a magic show about real magic and found ourselves reading works by many esoteric writers from the past and present. The writings of Carlos Castañeda, Aleister Crowley, Alice Bailey, Dion Fortune, and many others crossed our desks. Jeff found the work of modern writer Donald Michael Kraig to be especially inspiring, and many of the ideas from Kraig's book *Modern Magick* found their way into the show we created with the help of director Bob Fitch. Mask, Myth & Magic had its premiere off-Broadway at a club called The Ballroom in 1990. *New York Times* columnist Glenn Collins wrote, "Mr. McBride combines magic with mime, dance, Kabuki Theater and martial arts. He wields the primordial weapons of the magician—the wand, chalice and sword. He wrestles with titanic unseen forces. He does not do rabbits."

What is even more important in terms of the quest to become a wizard is the personal path Jeff set for himself in order to reach a point where he could create *Mask, Myth & Magic*. He purposely sought out new experiences for himself that would take him into situations where he had to grow and discover new aspects of himself. This willingness to stretch is one of the marks of a true wizard, for we can only discover the uncommon wisdom that will make us wizards by having and paying attention to experiences that force us to grow and change.

Not too long after Jeff started performing *Mask, Myth & Magic*, first in New York, then at casinos in Atlantic City and arts festivals in London, Hong Kong, and Taiwan, Jeff and I set out on a different kind of adventure that was to shape my ideas about magic and, ultimately, wizardry. He had a favorite saying: "You can't give a gift that you don't have." In keeping with this saying, it followed that if one has never had a true magical experience, one might have difficulty offering that experience to others. We both agreed that one of the primary functions of any magician ought to be to give his audiences a magical experience. And so, with the wonderful help of Eugene Burger, Bob Neale, Bob Fitch, and others, we created The Mystery School.

The Mystery School was an annual three-day retreat at which we attempted to give true magical experiences to other magicians. We created activities for those who attended, based on some of the experiences that Jeff had had on his various quests to find real magic. Drumming circles, wizard's walks, initiation rituals, and much more all took place. A community was created that, because of their deeply shared love for that vision of magic, continues to stay in touch even to this day. McBride's work with The Mystery School created a new movement in magic, such that London's Magic Circle, one of the oldest fraternities of magicians in the world, described him as "perhaps the most influential magician of our time."

Over the years, I've seen Jeff McBride truly and consciously transform himself from a young, angry hot-shot performer with a burning need to always be the center of attention into someone who not long ago could tell me, "Whether it's been Mystery School or World Magics or the Wonderdome or Burning Man installations or Vegas Vortex gatherings, it has all been different containers for exploring the same vision: bringing people together to support them in finding and empowering their own vision, to lead a more enriched and whole life. That's my greatest achievement." Even Jeff's shows have transformed. "I no longer want spectators; spectators are there to spectate—that is, to watch. And I don't want audiences, who are there to listen. I want participants, who come to party!" he said in a recent interview. His shows are now interactive, transformative experiences designed to transform both the performer and his audience. And that is true wizardry.

Sylvia Brallier

Time to get a little crazy.

So often we rein ourselves in in ways that really don't serve us. We get overly concerned about what other people will think, and in the process we lose opportunities to express ourselves and be a little freer, a little more creative, a little more uniquely ourselves.

— Sylvia Brallier[13]

Sylvia Brallier is a modern shaman and miracle worker. Throughout her life, she has dared to explore thoughts, ideas, and ways of being that are outside societal norms. As a result, she has collected a large store of secret knowledge, especially in the field of personal empowerment and healing techniques, which allows her to create amazing transformations in her clients and students.

I was first introduced to Sylvia by my friend Jeff McBride. He had been pursuing his quest to find real magic, seeking out experiences ranging from yoga retreats to Native American sweat lodges. He returned after one weekend's outing to proclaim, "I've found it! You won't believe what happened to me!" Jeff had attended one of Sylvia's transformational breath work ceremonies at an event called Rites of Spring, and it had been a truly mind-altering experience for him. He later became Sylvia's student, traveling back and forth between New York and her home in Western Massachusetts every time he had a few days free between jobs. Sylvia's knowledge and experience covered a wide range of esoteric yet practical subjects, much of which might well be termed "real magic." Her knowledge was won through her natural willingness to seek out and explore teachings and experiences most others would have foregone.

When Sylvia was a young child, both Uri Geller and the Amazing Kreskin were popular on television. Both purported to have unusual gifts, to be able to read minds, move objects, and bend metal using only the power of their mind. Of course, most of what they were doing was actually accomplished through the same kind of deception used by any stage conjurer. Not having experienced such trickery herself, Sylvia was determined to teach herself to do the things they did. She trained her powers of observation and embarked on a lifelong journey to develop her own intuitive abilities. Before long, she was actually doing the things she had seen the mentalists pretend to do on television— speaking with spirits, sensing what others were thinking and feeling with uncanny accuracy, and sometimes even influencing the current of events using only her mind—but without using the magician's trickery that the television performers used.

In addition to the seemingly mystical abilities she had developed, Sylvia studied Ericksonian hypnosis, and soon she began using all her knowledge to help others. She discovered that she could often have a profound effect by using her empathic abilities to treat and release people from the traumas and ways of thinking that were damaging their physical or emotional well-being.

Blessed with an active and curious mind, Sylvia felt compelled to figure out the rationale behind what she was able to do. As a result, she has been able to teach others how to develop and use those abilities, and she also has been able to speak and write about them in a clear and rational way. Having gained her own "powers" through her willingness to experience what others would not, along with her willingness to see the world from many different perspectives, she dedicates her time to helping and empowering others.

Many of the techniques revealed in this book are versions of practices I have learned in my own studies with Sylvia.

George Parker

> *I think a Wizard is a master at 'changing reality at will'. And that's what I practice in my life. This sounds simple and it ultimately is. But it's not easy.*

George Parker[14]

A true modern wizard, George Parker performs magic shows that transform his audiences. He has worked as a programmer, teacher, author, trainer, consultant and in several other roles over the course of his life. A few years ago, he decided to invent a new kind of career and dubbed himself a "corporate alchemist." Using skills developed over many years, George ascertains the problems that his clients—usually businesses—are experiencing and then uses his wisdom to figure out the transformations necessary for those clients to resolve their problems. He then creates experiences—often in the form of shows or lectures—that will bring them to the point where they are ready for the transformations required. Because George's work is so effective, it is in high demand throughout Europe. He has to turn down as many engagements as he accepts, and many clients engage him again and again once they have experienced what he does.

George was kind enough to spend a great deal of time answering questions for this book, so you will find many quotes and stories from him throughout these pages. If the description I have provided here seems a bit short, don't worry. We will be getting to know George Parker quite well in the chapters to come.

Eve Ensler

> *...find freedom, aliveness, and power not from what contains, locates, or protects us, but from what dissolves, reveals, and expands us.*

Eve Ensler[15]

Eve Ensler is an award-winning playwright and activist in the movement to stop violence against women. While there have been many playwrights and theater movements whose goal was to effect political change, Ensler's approach is unique—and a perfect example of true wizardry in action.

It begins with the willingness to think and act as a renegade, to go against the grain. Ensler's play *The Vagina Monologues* was written in 1996 and first performed in the basement of the Cornelia Street Café in Greenwich Village. The play is an episodic collection of women's monologues about, to quote Wikipedia, "the feminine experience, touching on matters such as sex, love, rape, menstruation, female genital mutilation, masturbation, birth, orgasm, the various common names for the vagina. A recurring theme throughout the piece is the vagina as a tool of female empowerment, and the ultimate embodiment of individuality." Even in the generally progressive world of New York theater, these were not comfortable ideas. The performances shocked audiences and forced them to confront their own attitudes and prejudices. Ensler's courage in writing and performing the play was rewarded with sold-out audiences and multiple awards.

Her remarkable play isn't the main reason Eve Ensler is included in this book, though. Being a playwright capable of moving your audiences doesn't necessarily make you a wizard. Many artists are renegade thinkers to some extent or another. What Ensler chose to do with her play after its initial set of award-winning performances is what really sets her apart.

Once the initial run of their play has ended, most playwrights follow a tried-and-true path of licensing their script to other groups. Regional theaters, theaters in other countries, community groups, and others pay royalties in exchange for the license to perform the playwright's work, and the playwright thus derives an ongoing income from her work for many years after the initial production closes.

Ensler chose a different path. She set up the V-Day movement. Each year, for several weeks surrounding February 14, groups around the world declare V-Day and perform *The Vagina Monologues* with a volunteer cast and crew, usually as a benefit for a local women's shelter, a rape crisis center, or a similar organization. The performances become the centerpiece for festivals celebrating women artists, craftswomen, and feminist activism. Ensler does not receive royalties.

To the best of my knowledge, no other playwright has committed to this kind of arrangement, in which they not only donate what would otherwise be their royalties from a production but also use the occasion of each production as the centerpiece of a social activist movement. Ensler's approach makes her play the leverage point for activating a movement that continues to generate major media attention and raise monies for her cause. The performances certainly succeed in moving their audience, but the arrangement through which Ensler has seen that her play will be performed does so much more. Year after year, whole communities become involved. Funds are raised and distributed. Stories appear in the media, keeping the issues before the public. All of these events occur because Ensler was able to look at the business of being a playwright from a different perspective and had the courage to take a different path. Ensler accepted personal responsibility for changing the world in which she lives and chose to take uncommon action to make changes in that world. Her vision, her courage, and her willingness to take responsibility and take action all mark Eve Ensler as a true wizard.

Closing the Gallery

Now that we have met a few wizards, let's have a look at what these individuals have in common that might be different from the rest of us. What special skills, knowledge, and ways of thinking give them their special powers? How did they develop these powers? Most important, how can you develop your own wizardly powers?

Let's start here: Wizards gain wisdom by seeking out and creating experiences (learning opportunities) and then reflecting on those experiences. They place a high value on firsthand experience both as a vehicle for changing themselves and as a way to obtain the master skills and knowledge they need to change the world. Wizards actively seek their own vision, often by observing the world more acutely and from more perspectives than others. They use their unique perspectives to find leverage points they can use to create large changes with relatively little effort. Wizards also learn to view the world as systems operating within larger systems—again, with leverage points that can create change in the larger systems as a result of smaller changes in the smaller systems. A creative mind-set combined with the principle of radical responsibility propels wizards to actively create change in the world. Learning meta-skills allows wizards to rapidly reap maximum benefit from secret knowledge gained through both study and experience, which in turn allows them to consciously change themselves and thereby change the world around them. They use the power of words, role-playing, secret knowledge, and many other techniques, always with the awareness that change in the world around us begins with change in ourselves.

In the chapters that follow, we will examine each of these principles in further detail, learning about them from the experiences of our many wizard models. You will learn simple exercises you can do in order to begin using these principles in your own life. I am confident that by the time you finish this book, you will find yourself well on the road to becoming a real wizard, wielding powers you never dreamed you could have. Abracadabra!

Notes

1.   Rob Siltanen with participation of Lee Clow, both of Chiat\Day, the advertisement for the "Think Different Campaign" of Apple, Inc. 2008

2.   White, T.H. *The Once and Future King*, page 168

3.   White, T.H. *The Book of Merlyn*

4.   Rowling, J.K. *Harry Potter and the Sorcerer's Stone*, page 157

5.   Tolkien, J.R.R., *The Fellowship of the Ring*, page 351

6.   This from the original *Wizard of Oz* film script, which I can find only in digital format. No page number available.

7.   From *The Notebooks of Leonardo da Vinci*, edited and translated by Edward MacCurdy, page 57

8.   Brockman, John, *My Einstein*, page 6, reporting on a letter Einstein wrote to Mileva Maric

9.   Gandhi, Mohandas. No direct source can be found for this widely quoted saying, but it is widely attributed to Gandhi.

10.	Zell-Ravenheart, Oberon *Grimoire for the Apprentice Wizard*, page 6, 2004

11.	Jobs, Steve, Commencement Address at Stanford, 2005. Available here: http://news.stanford.edu/news/2005/june15/jobs-061505.html

12.	McBride, Jeff The Museletter, March 2014. The Museletter is a newsletter published twice monthly to subscribers. It is also archived at http://blog.mcbridemagic.com

13.	From Sylvia Brallier's Blog: http://sylviabrallier.com/blog/

14.	From an unpublished interview with George Parker, conducted by the author.

15.	Ensler, Eve *Insecure at Last, Losing It in Our Security-Obsessed World*, Introduction, page xx, 2006

Finding Your Vision

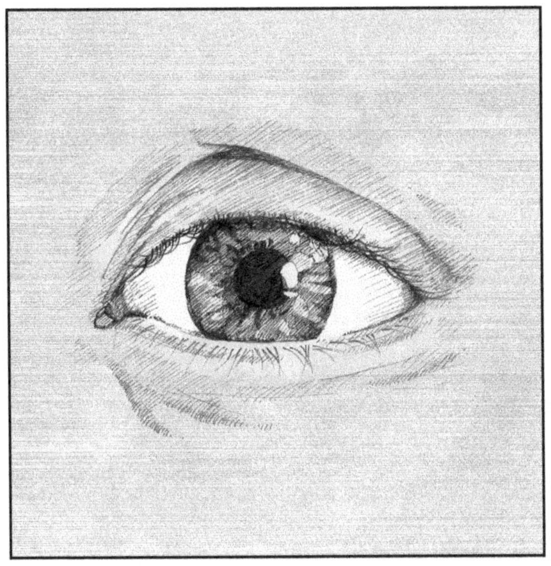

IT'S ABOUT TIME.

MARELI SMIT

To Theo, Eben, and Louis. You make my time on earth matter. May your most significant fears become your biggest celebrations.

To my cheerleaders — you always inspire me and give me the courage to push through.

"Don't wait for the stars to align. Reach up, rearrange them the way you want them to be. Create your own constellation."

– Pharrell Williams

FOREWORD

When looking at the regrets of the dying, they regret the things they never did instead of regretting some of the dumbass things they did do. This book teaches you how to live without regrets, make sure you abundantly live a full life, and make the best use of your time.

Time is our most precious, scarcest, and unpredictably limited resource. This book teaches you how to befriend, overcome, and intimately get to know your fears and perceived limitations so that you can move through them instead of giving them the power to shut doors on what you are yearning for in life.

I am grateful for every piece of music, art and innovation created after the creators overcame fear and chose to birth something with a profound message. To all the future artists, creators, innovators, and authors, I pray that you overcome your fears and befriend and tame those inner voices warning you about looking like a fool. To all of you afraid to leap, please read this book!

I am grateful to Mareli, the beautiful, vibrant and loving author of this book, but also my best friend, colleague and soul sister, for pushing through when every bone in her body doubted herself. You are not a bracket; you are an exclamation mark! Inside joke about what we would be if we were a punctuation mark!

To all reading this, live your life in such a way that when you die, the world cries and you rejoice about a life well lived. This book will help you rejoice about how you spend your time!

Chantel Botha, Author of "The Customer Journey Mapping Field Guide" and the founder of BrandLove.

ACKNOWLEDGEMENT.

A special thanks goes to everyone who inspired, guided, mentored, pushed, and contributed to my growth and continue to do so! Thank you to Karlien Botha, Colleen Lightbody, Ryan Stramrod, and Rosaria Cirillo Louwman for the insights and stories included in this book. Thank you to my colleagues and friends at Brandlove who make the world better, one interaction at a time. Thank you to my parents, Helgaard and Bessie for loving and supporting me ALWAYS. A huge thank you to Theo, my biggest cheerleader, friend, soulmate, and love of my life. Last but not least, to my sons, Eben and Louis, you inspire me to be better. I love you to the moon and back.

PREFACE.

Let's clarify this from the get-go. This is not a self-help – there-is-something-wrong-with-you-that-you-need-to-fix kind of book. This is an excuse my French, 'own your shit' book. We are human and messy, and life is a roller coaster ride. The question is – are you just along for the ride or are you invested to add new tracks and routes to this roller coaster ride called life?

Many hopes and dreams are floating around, hidden, and forgotten in a drawer somewhere. An idea scribbled on a piece of paper or a vision, dream, or excitement about something buried deep within our hearts. Covered in cobwebs and dust. I will be the first to confess that this is a hard truth to hear. Maybe like me, you tell yourself it is okay. Life happened. I don't have time for this right now. Maybe one day. I will still get to it. I am still young, or lately, it is too late to start now. But maybe the worst of it all is letting other people prioritise what you achieve or don't achieve.

So, it never happens. Those dreams and ideas stay just that – dreams and ideas.

I wonder what the real reason is that we opt out of our dreams? What are the fears and beliefs or stories we tell ourselves that overpower and dim our spark?

I know now that people who have their dreams come true are mostly those who made a choice to prioritise it, work hard, and MAKE it happen. It does not happen by chance. They are not just lucky. It takes work. It takes time. It takes blood, sweat and tears. Listen, if reading this scares you a bit or sounds like effort, please push through. That is exactly the emotion you need to get traction and to change. No change was ever born from contentment, comfort or inaction! In the words of my first boss: "If you get comfortable, it is time to get uncomfortable!"

The cost of not following your dream is always regret.

Think about this. The athlete who wins that Olympic gold. That entrepreneur who starts to expand their business and opens their first official office. That chef who gets a Michelin star – it all started with an idea. A dream. A vision followed by A LOT OF EFFORT AND TIME.

So, why would it be any different for anything else in life? Not always the BIG extreme things like the Olympics or Michelin star but living life on your own terms. Doing the things that give you joy. To get the most out of life with no regrets when you get to the end of your life. To contribute to people around you by being the best version of you. Whatever that looks like for you.

Imagine you meet your future self today. The person you could have become. What would they say to you?

This is the moment.

You have a choice.

Choose!

Choose an extraordinary life!

You can live a default life, continue believing your own excuses, and see what happens. Staying a spectator. And it may well be a wonderful life. BUT what if it could be an extraordinary life? What if you could move from a default state to a design and action state, living the life you've been dreaming of?

Stop being a spectator and choose to become a real participator!

I encourage you to make a choice.

Prioritise you.

Make the time and take the time to fully commit to you, so that there is more of you to give to the world.

It's About Freaking Time for you – don't you think?

Let me tell you a story.

I remember how my mom taught me the basics of cooking when I was old enough to care. She taught me how to slice an onion for a delicious stew. She showed me how to make custard to accompany one of her steamy baked puddings. She made a home-cooked meal look like no effort at all. When I got my own place and had to cook meals to impress my boyfriend, I got to know Jamie Oliver, a talented English chef. I sat for hours with my notebook and watched his cooking shows on a Sunday afternoon every week - this was before Netflix, and then tried the recipes out for myself with great success. I felt inspired and confident – equipped with tips and practical ideas that set me up for success while adding value to my food experiences. As I became more confident, understanding the basics of flavours and combinations, I experimented with new ideas and flavours. I can now open the refrigerator, see what ingredients I have, and create excellent meals. This gives me immense joy!

This book, however, is not a book about cooking or food, but rather a food-for-thought book, using food and recipes as an analogy. I am not a chef. Nor am I close to being an expert. I am terrible at plating food, but flavour trumps looks, in my opinion. However, what I am good at is looking at the ingredients I have available and creating the best possible meal I can. It energises me – to touch, taste, smell, and appreciate food.

But what is even more satisfying is if the people enjoying my food light up and feel fulfilled. If I can bring a smile to their faces, I've achieved my goal.

To make a great meal, you need the best ingredients, spices, tools, kitchen space, a good knife, utensils, and in most cases, electricity, gas, or fire. To take a meal from ordinary to extraordinary requires planning, focus, inspiration, creativity, and time.

The same applies to life. Are you living an everyday functional life that is acceptable to most, or do you crave an extraordinary life filled with explosions of tastes, colour, and aromas?

Is your life like take-out - fast and convenient, but bland, fine dining - overcomplicated, but tasteful, or home-cooked - fulfilling and shared with loved ones?

I've put together a menu of life recipes, ideas, tips, and tool suggestions that may help you find the ingredients, inspiration, focus, and confidence to create a life that you long to have. Everything I selected for you as ingredients to life in this book is what I wish I had known as my younger self. I hope you can make it your own and that it will add more flavour and depth to your life. Most people have the best intentions to live a fulfilling life, but it is easy to fall into the trap of living a default life. To go on autopilot and see where life takes you. I believe that there is a different way. That you can design how you want to live and experience life.

You are ultimately the master chef of your own life.

One thing is certain – things will go right, and things will go wrong. But when you get that one meal perfect, it is immensely satisfying. Accept that it will not always go your way.

You will fail. You will feel frustrated. The electricity will sometimes go off, or the gas might run out. But the trick is to try and try again. Life is not a sprint but a marathon.

I've realised that the constant in the meal analogy is TIME. It takes time to plan and to cook. It takes great timing to get all the food on the plate while it is still hot.

My invitation is this: Take the time to figure out what is missing from your life 'meal' or how to spice up an already wonderful life. Choose ingredients to add your unique flavour.

Stop living a default life and start living an extraordinary life you design!

INTRODUCTION.

It's about TIME.

Allow me to be your guide on this Discovery, Design and Doing journey.

TIME to design your life.

Welcome to your life workbook.

Let me be straight with you. This is not a 'lie back and fall asleep with this book on your face' type of read. It is an investment in yourself to become the best version of you. To fully stand in your power and own your life. To ignite your magic and superpowers that you bring to the world. It will not happen by chance. It will take time and effort. It is your choice if you will make time for you. I will never ask you to do anything I did not also do. It is up to you how much effort you will put in. But, if you do want real change, I ask that you follow the process, do the exercises and be open-minded. You are worthy of an investment of your time!

Look at the following statements and answer it truthfully:

1. I sometimes feel that I am living a life that is directly affected or

   influenced by people, circumstances, or my environment.

Yes ☐   No ☐

2. My fears, beliefs or assumptions get in the way of my dreams.

Yes ☐   No ☐

3. I am on autopilot at work or at home or feel stuck in a rut.

Yes ☐   No ☐

4. I feel like a failure when I have the best intentions to start something positive in life, but every single time something seems to get in the way.

Yes ☐   No ☐

5. I sometimes wonder what my life purpose really is.

Yes ☐   No ☐

6. I am happy, but I want to take life to the next level.

Yes ☐   No ☐

If you answered yes to any of the above, you are ready for this journey! It is time to take the time for **YOU!**

It is time to reignite your values, authenticity, and authority.

Think about creating a delicious meal.

First, you need a vision of what the meal will look and taste like. Then you need to find a suitable recipe. Then you follow the recipe, adding one ingredient at a time. You need to plan your timing to ensure the food is ready and warm when you dish it up for your family or guests.

The same applies to your life. To create a life you dream of and desire, you need clarity around your vision for yourself, a plan, and a schedule allowing you to fully stand in your power. It may take a lot of willpower, courage and commitment. But in the end, the reward of a designed life is so worth the time spent on not only dreaming it and designing it but also becoming it!

Before we embark on this journey, here are some guidelines to make your journey more pleasant:

Principle 1: Be kind. Do not rush or judge yourself or others.

Principle 2: Choose to prioritise your life and commit to yourself.

Principle 3: Be open to the opportunities that may be right in front of you, even if you can't see them yet.

Principle 4: Give yourself permission to try and fail, but never fail to try.

Principle 5: Change your 'have to do' or 'must do' to 'get to do'. To live is an honour, a gift and a blessing.

Principle 6: Refer back to steps 1–5

Design the life you've always dreamed about and then find ways to make it happen.

Dream it. Design it. And DO it.

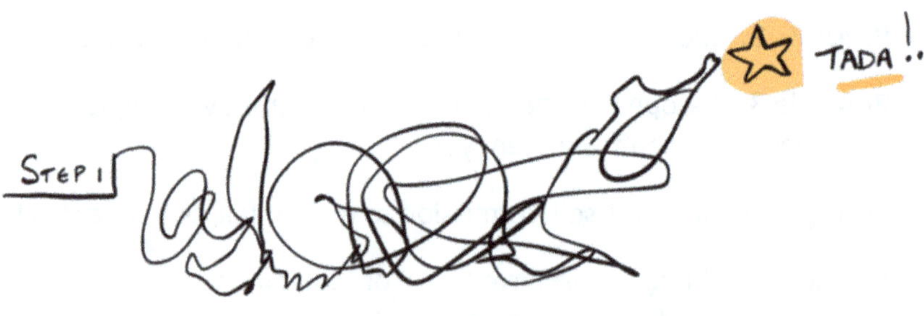

Real-time design

How to use this book.

I know that you are curious and probably want to jump straight into reading. I want to invite you to take your time when reading this book. Do not rush. Do not speed read it.

1.   Spend time on one chapter at a time.

2.   See this as a workbook. Your life guidebook. Do the work and let it sink in before moving on to the next chapter. You will find a ME TIME section for self-reflection, worksheets and note-taking in each chapter. Get a dedicated journal to keep notes.

3.   Take the time to unpack the content that speaks to you in detail.

4.   Answer the questions truthfully – suspend all judgement and notice your inner critic - that critical and negative voice in your head and heart telling you 'you can't do it' or 'you are not good enough,' for instance. This inner critic's job is to protect you, and it takes its job very seriously, especially when change is imminent. Recognise the critic, comfort it, tell it you are okay, and then send it on holiday while you do your work.

5.   Do the exercises and be mindful while spending time on these pages. When you physically write on a page rather than type on a keyboard, you allow for deeper and more critical thinking, so use a pen and paper if possible.

6.   Let it sink in. Reflect. Try things out. Challenge yourself.

7.   Prioritise your own growth. Remember that you are whole and resourceful.

8.   Do not stop at design but action it! If you want to shift to a design rather than a default mindset, put in the work and time. Remember that whatever you desire will need to be actioned. Life is a DOing word.

You've got this!

I.

DISCOVER THE TRUE YOU.

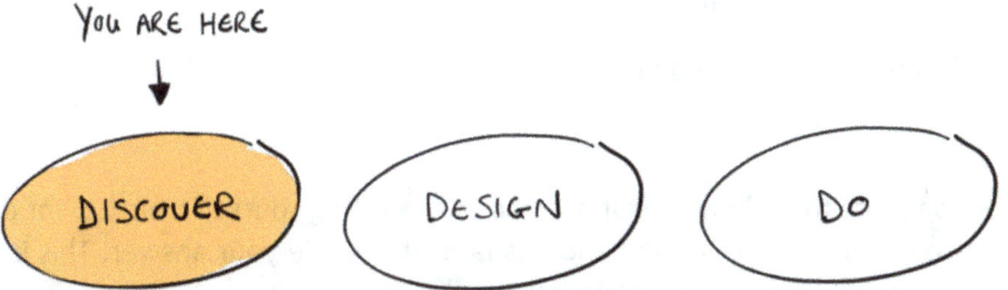

In this section, we will evaluate how you spend your time and what emotions occupy your life. At the end of this section, you will have clarity on what you want most in life and what may be getting in the way of it.

In this self-assessment we will look at the following areas:

A – assess where you are now and where you want to be and focus on the right things

B – believe that you can

O – out with the old beliefs, in with the fresh beliefs

U – understand your why and why not

T – think about who you are and how you want to show up in this world

T – take ownership of your life

I – include the people and things that give you joy

M – make it happen

E – embrace every moment

Complete the following self-assessment by rating yourself from 1-5 for each area, where 1 is not good and 5 is fantastic. Circle your answer. This is the time to be brutally honest with yourself!

1. How happy am I with my life today?

    1.   2.   3.   4.   5.

2. Am I focusing on what will bring me closer to living my desired life?

    1.   2.   3.   4.   5.

3. How confident do I feel that I will reach my dreams?

   1.   2.   3.   4.   5.

4. How open am I to changing the beliefs that keeps me away from my dreams?

   1.   2.   3.   4.   5.

5. I know and understand my purpose in life

   1.   2.   3.   4.   5.

6. I know who I am and how I want to show up in this world

   1.   2.   3.   4.   5.

7. I allow others to prioritise what I achieve or don't achieve in life

   1.   2.   3.   4.   5.

8. I have people in my life that bring me joy

   1.   2.   3.   4.   5.

9. I make things happen and own my own happiness

   1.   2.   3.   4.   5.

10. I embrace every moment and make the most of it – in good times and bad times

   1.   2.   3.   4.   5.

Now journal on the following questions:

1. What is it that I want most from life?

2. Why is this important for me?

3. What is the commitment I am making to myself in this moment?

CHAPTER 1.

BECOME A MASTER OF TIME.

Time; what a fantastic concept. We all have 86 400 seconds, 1 140 minutes, 24 hours a day, seven days a week, 52 weeks or 365 days a year. And still, somehow, it seems we never have enough time.

This book is an attempt to remind you that you are amazing. If you choose, you have time to design the life that you dream of and desire. Isn't it about time that you realise that whatever happens in life is not happening to you, but for you? Allowing you to learn, grow and be the best 'you' that you can be.

It's about time for you to shine!

TIME is relative.

When I started to write this book, the world was very different. Everyone, including me, had many excuses for not having enough time. Then a pandemic forced us all to re-evaluate how we spend our time.

Some rediscovered how precious time is. Some realised that time is just a construct of our imagination. Some lost time, some found time. Lockdown was a reset button for me – almost as if the universe sent us all to our rooms to rethink our lives.

The funny thing about having time to think is that you have two choices: you can either grab the opportunity to connect with yourself and others or disconnect and put your head in the sand by using avoidance tactics.

Disconnecting tactics may include, but are not limited to, mind-numbing activities like binge-watching your favourite series, eating, drinking, or sleeping.

As mentioned before, when you connect with yourself, you are bound to meet your inner critic. That inner voice that can sometimes be mean and vicious. It is usually shaped throughout our lives, creating our internal stories or narratives; this critical voice in our heads and hearts, feeding us lies like 'you are not good enough' or 'you are not worthy' or 'you will never be able to do that'. The interesting thing is that this saboteur is merely doing its job. Its job is to protect us from getting hurt or embarrassing ourselves. And although the intention is good, the outcome is that it stops us from leaning into things that are good for us. It gives us a reason to cop out, not commit fully, and an excuse not to be brave. Being vulnerable scares us all. Facing our fears is not easy.

Although I do not have a PhD or degree in time, quantum physics, or science, I am sure if there was a degree in the 'I do not have enough time excuse to avoid stuff degree', I would pass, cum laude.

"I am so busy at work, I have no time to run anymore." or "I am so busy balancing work and home-life that I do not have time for coffee with my friends." or "I have no time to write that book about fear I've been saying I would write for the past five years."

Sound familiar? Is it true? Would I be able to make time if I prioritised it? And lately, what do I choose to make time for?

Our time reality[1].

We segment our lives into three parts to make sense of our time on Earth: What happened in the past, what is happening in the present, and what might happen in the future. We then operate and experience different perspectives, depending on where we focus. Like most things in life, there is a light and dark side to all three perspectives. Let's unpack it in a bit more detail.

Past-focused.
When we are past-focused, we focus on positive and negative things that happened in the past that impacted our experiences. These experiences

---

[1] Sive.rs. 2009. *The Time Paradox – by Philip Zimbardo and John Boyd | Derek Sivers*. [online] Available at: <https://sive.rs/book/TimeParadox>.

create the core of our future selves. When we spend time thinking of past experiences, we can learn and reflect on them, and make different choices. But, if we got hurt or failed in the past, it can limit us from trying new things, because we are scared to get hurt again. We armour ourselves as best we can and will do almost anything to avoid pain at all costs.

This thinking becomes our belief - what we think is true even without proof and we behave or react in a certain way because of what we believe.

Let's unpack an example to illustrate this. Sam was happily married for 10 years. Then, suddenly, without warning, Sam's spouse died. Traumatised by this event, Sam struggled to move past it. After a couple of years and with the support of family and friends, Sam started online dating, going out and meeting new people. Sam met many new people that were awesome and that she could be happy with and even build a new life with. But, after a couple of months Sam always found a reason to end the relationship. Her strong belief that "she will never find anyone as great as her husband" drives her behaviour. The only remedy is if Sam changes her belief from "no one will ever be as good as my husband" to something like "I deserve love even if it is not the same as I had before". Only then will she be able to let go of, and move past, the hurt and be open to receiving love and connection in the future. There is nothing wrong with reflecting on the past. For Sam it is holding on to precious memories and the love of her life. It is, however, important to understand that what we focus on will become our story. If we look at past experiences with a curiosity lens on and find nuggets to help us understand ourselves better, it is a true gift. We may never truly understand why things turned out the way it did, but if we can let go of what keeps us from moving forward, it is a true gift.

Future-focused.

When we are future-focused, with both positive and negative thoughts of what the future may hold, we can either limit or create wings for ourselves. Let's unpack the light and dark side of being only future-focused.

People who are focused only on the future, sometimes give up essential time with the people they love, as they are working hard to fulfil their future vision. They tend to not prioritise fun, hobbies, or even sleep. Future-focused people usually strive for work, achievement, and control. It is great to have a vision and work hard at it, but if this is the only focus, it may lead to burnout. If someone is negatively future-focused, they are generally anxious and continually worry about what could potentially go wrong. Looking forward could be great – especially if you have a vision for yourself.

But, having a wonderful one-day-I-will attitude fosters procrastination in the now. It is essential to have balance.

Present-focused.

Present-focused people tend to have the energy to try new things, be mindful, and find joy in the present. They live only for the moment and enjoy themselves here and now. They may even lose themselves in time. This process is called going into a state of flow[2] which usually happens when people are busy with an activity where they are totally immersed and focused and where their ego falls away and time flies by. Imagine the last time you were busy with something you loved or enjoyed doing, only to realise that three hours had passed, but it felt like 20 minutes. For some, this happens when they create artwork, exercise or even cook a great meal for their family. That is what it feels like to be in a state of flow. Present-focused people seem to focus more on helping others than themselves, which can also become a problem in and of itself.

The trick is to have a healthy balance between all three perspectives.

Live a holistic life in the present and include and be curious about past and future perspectives.

---

[2] Snyder, C., Lopez, S., Edwards, L. and Marques, S., 2021. *The Oxford Handbook of Positive Psychology*. Oxford: Oxford University Press USA - OSO, pp.195-203.

Where do you spend your time?

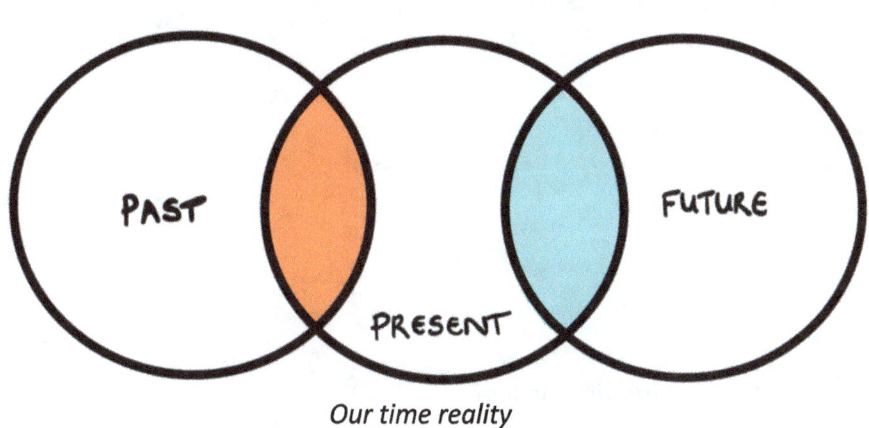

Our time reality

Time travel in balance assessment.

Take a moment. Pause. And think – where do you spend most of your time?

How much time traveling, do you do to the past? ☐ %

How much time traveling do you do to the future? ☐ %

How much time are you present in the moment? ☐ %

Look at your rating and reflect on the following questions:

1. Where is my focus?

2. What do I prioritise in life?

3. Is there anything I can do differently to get more balance?

Time travel in balance.

People who get stuck in a constant state of regret of what happened in the past or live in a state of fear of the unknown future really struggle to see and embrace the present state. This impacts our ability to see opportunities that present themselves daily. We become blind to the things right in front of us. Remember that we ultimately become what we focus on.

Do you know someone who always finds the negative in ANY situation? Or a person who finds a way to smile or laugh no matter what happens in life?

Positive people will focus on the positive, and negative people will focus on the negative. And that will become their reality.

I am not saying you should never reflect on the past or unpack the future. It would be unwise not to spend some time reflecting. But choose what you will focus on. And decide what gold and learning you will take from past mistakes, experiences, or situations. Or if you will decide to see future problems as problems or opportunities.

I have a friend who continually reminds me to find the gold in situations gone wrong. The Japanese take this literally with their Kintsugi[3] or Kintsukuroi artform, where they use a special tree sap lacquer, dusted with powdered gold, to rejoin and repair broken ceramic pieces. It celebrates brokenness rather than hiding it.

I wish we could do the same! I wish we could teach our kids that 'failure' is a gift of learning and that there is not always just a right or wrong way. There is, however, a choice to make.

What will you focus on?

What emotions dominate your life?

Even though we see ourselves as rational humans who make decisions based on facts alone, we are mistaken. We may think this is true, but what really drives our behaviours are emotions. Emotion is the driving force that can either hold us back or propel us forward. The sooner we realise and embrace this, the better for us and the people around us!

---

[3] Manzella, K., 2022. *Kintsugi – Art of Repair | Traditional Kyoto*. [online] Traditionalkyoto.com. Available at: <https://traditionalkyoto.com/culture/kintsugi/>.

There are so many emotions described in the English language. But we use around 12 categories of emotions labelled by Caroll Izard from the University of Delaware in his 'Differential Emotions scale' as follows[4]: Interest, Joy, Surprise, Sadness, Anger, Disgust, Contempt, Self-Hostility, Fear, Shame, Shyness and Guilt. The interesting thing about these categories of emotions is that more than half make us feel terrible. We also lack the capacity to describe our emotions, so many people would describe their experiences as sad, mad or glad.

I find it bizarre that the thing that drives behaviour the most is also the thing that we are all trying to dodge or avoid at all costs. Firstly, we do not have the vocabulary to describe our emotions, we do not recognise the manifestation of these emotions in our bodies, and we avoid them as best we can – especially the not-so-positive emotions. And in our defense, it is not really our fault. It is the human condition. Since birth, we have been taught to avoid emotions. Think about the following: when a baby cries, we soothe it. When a toddler falls and cries, we give it ice cream to stop it from crying and distract it from the pain. When someone goes through a break-up, we take them out for a drink to numb the pain or offer someone a tissue, subliminally sending the message that they should stop crying. But this also applies to positive emotions. When someone achieves something, they may feel uncomfortable celebrating too much as they can be seen as boastful or egocentric. Too happy is also frowned upon. Crazy right? We avoid our emotions instead of experiencing them. We do not feel comfortable with our own emotions, let alone other people's emotions – both perceived positive and negative.

Whether we ignore or acknowledge the emotion, the emotion is always there. It is a form of energy, and we can proactively decide where to channel this energy. To do that, we first need to fully acknowledge and connect with the emotion. Rather than living a limited life, we should embrace the good, the bad and the ugly as if through the eyes of an open and expansive child.

Have a look at the illustrations to follow. The first image speaks to possibility and the second to a limited life because of the messages we receive throughout our lifetime.

---

[4] 2022. *Discrete emotion theory* [online] Wikipedia. Available at: https://en.wikipedia.org/wiki/Discrete_emotion_theory

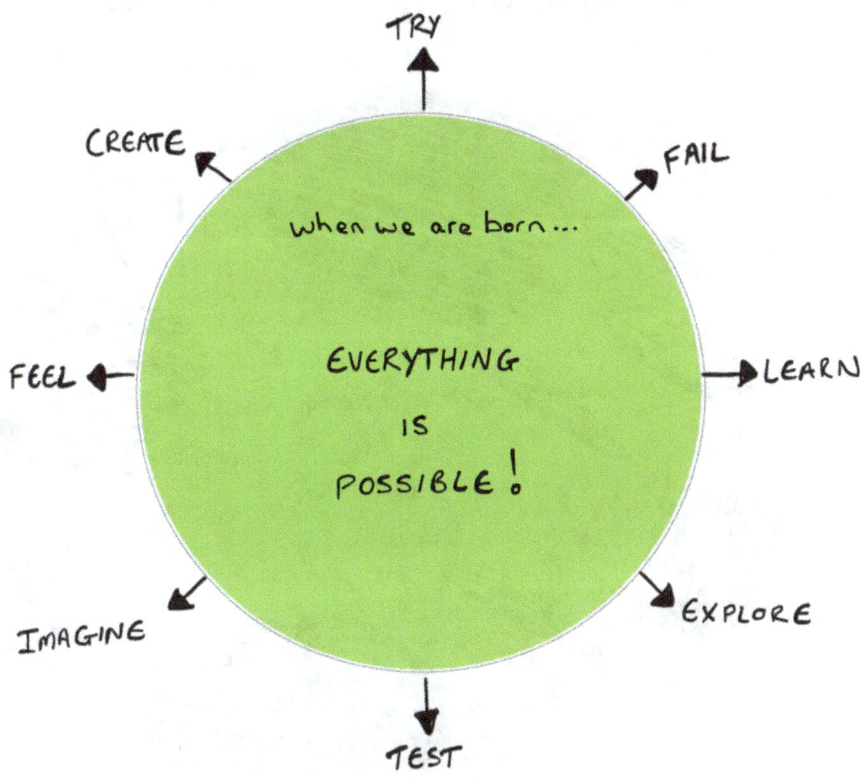

Everything is possible.

Then Life Happens...

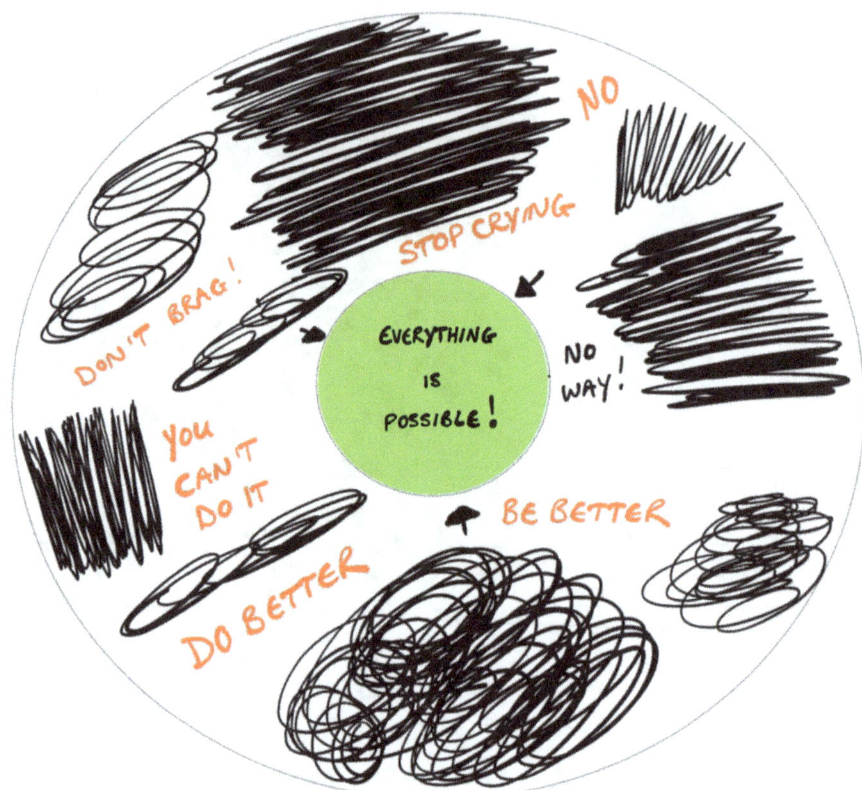

Limited lives.

My latest golden nugget I heard someone say was: "Everything gets to be. You get to be sad or glad or mad in the moment. You get to experience the energy in this moment".

Recipe for embracing emotional energy – a guide for yourself and others.

Step 1: Acknowledge the feeling. Give it a name.

Step 2: Really feel it in your body. Where does it sit in your body? Imagine the colour and shape of this feeling in your body.

Step 3: Sit with the feeling and really feel its energy even if it is uncomfortable.

Step 4: Make a choice. You can stay in this energy or choose to move through it.

Next time someone has an emotion, rather than trying to fix it or control the situation, sit next to them, and hold a space for them to feel what they feel. Give the emotion some space, time and attention. This is the greatest gift we can give.

On the other hand, let's say someone says something or does something that triggers an emotion in you; it is important to realise that you have a choice. You can either react with a reptile brain reaction that is not rational and a survival mechanism. This is called fight, flight or freeze mode. You may react by fighting with your words or physically, you can run away or excuse yourself to go to the bathroom to flee, or you can freeze by not reacting at all. With practice, you can however, react from either this reptile response place, or choose to take a breath and respond. Responding is identifying and then choosing to control or own the emotion and to set a boundary if needs be.

Let me give you an example. Let's say someone tells me that I am immature. My first reaction is that I want to defend my honour and attack (fight) – this is my emotional state, triggered by the other person. Instead, I identify the feeling and set a boundary with the person that may sound like this. "When you call me immature, you make me feel 'less than' and that makes me angry and sad at the same time". *(Name the feeling.)* "Please can you be a bit more sensitive next time?" *(Set the boundary.)*

INSIDE OUT PROCESS

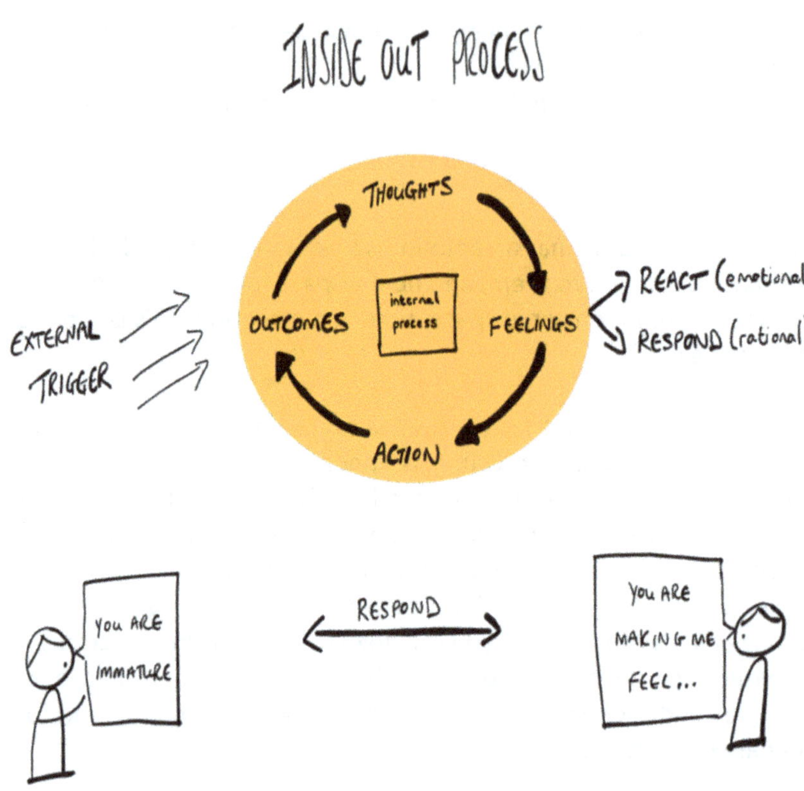

Our internal interpretation and actions we choose.

Now that you better understand where you spend your time and how emotions impact your behaviour, you can decide if you want to stay where you are or shift gears to set yourself up for success. Are you open to possibilities or are you limiting yourself?

* * *

Me Time.

It is now time to reflect. I've added some questions to guide you, allowing you to discover more about yourself.

Use the template on the next page to make notes and add additional notes in your journal should you need more thinking and writing space.

Reflect on the following questions and complete the worksheet:

1. What do I choose to focus on? Can I recognise any patterns?

2. How would my life be different if I acknowledged, learned from, but did not get stuck in the past?

3. How would my life be different if I identified, understood and accepted my fears but did not fixate on them?

4. How would my life and relationships be different if I made more time for the present and started enjoying what is right in front of me?

5. What emotions dominate my life?

6. How can I start choosing emotions?

7. What emotion do I feel right now? Where does it sit in my body? (Really feel it, experience it, and choose what you want to do next.)

Now that you had a chance to reflect, complete the worksheet on the next page.

PAST	PRESENT	FUTURE

How much **TIME**   %.   %.   %.   do I spend here?

↑IMPACT↑   ↑IMPACT↑   ↑IMPACT↑

EMOTIONS: ______   EMOTIONS: ______   EMOTIONS: ______

What would life be like if I could leave this behind?

How can I do more of this?

How can I get this to serve me, not limit me?

CHAPTER 2.

HOW STORIES LIMIT AND EXPAND US.

Telling stories around the dinner table was always my favourite time when growing up: listening to the adults talk about things that did not always make sense to me; the laughter and reminiscence about past holidays or funny situations; sharing ideas and checking in with each other after a busy day.

Dinner time is still sacred to me. We sit together as a family to enjoy meals regularly. For me, this is a time to connect. And I hope that I can instil this tradition in my boys. They may not understand the impact yet, but my wish for them is that they will get to understand the power of family time and continue this tradition with their families one day.

Storytelling plays such a vital role in our reality and in how we perceive ourselves and others. Those stories around dinner time when I was growing up formed my worldview and how I perceive the world, others, and myself. It influenced my inner voice or narrative as well. Stories, in my mind, are the things that can either positively or negatively affect our lives. It is also important to first understand our current stories to be able to craft our new stories.

To understand storytelling, however, we need to start at the beginning. Like most good stories, this one also begins with: Once upon a time …

The brief history of storytelling.

Storytelling is as old as humankind. Since our brains are visually wired, drawings have always been an effective way to tell stories about survival and life. The Egyptian hieroglyphics used pictographic characters as symbols. Many tribes used cave drawings that focused on sharing hunting stories.

Another form of sharing stories was through music and drama. The writers skillfully used characters and elaborate plots to help spice things up and keep audiences engaged in their stories. People told stories around campfires in many parts of the world, passing on traditions from one generation to the next.

Written stories followed much later, and readership was limited to a select few. Plays made stories more accessible to a broader audience – literacy was meant only for the educated. But this changed in the 15th century, when Johannes Gutenberg invented the printing press, allowing mass accessibility to printed material. However, the Chinese monks printed their Buddhist scripture, the Diamond Sutra,[5] using a block printing mechanism that set ink to paper using wooden blocks 600 years before Gutenberg.

Photographs captured moments, and technology brought us moving pictures, the TV, and the internet. These mediums allowed people to identify with what they saw on screen and created a vast aspirational drive. Heroes and influencers were born, and people aspired to be like, dress like or live like the celebrities they saw on screen.

Today, technology is growing exponentially, and people instantly have access to each other's stories, leading to the overexposure and bombardment of messages from all angles. There are a lot of choices, but also a lot of noise.

---

[5] Wikipedia Contributors, 2019. *Diamond Sutra*. [online]. Wikipedia. Available at: <https://en.wikipedia.org/wiki/Diamond_Sutra>.

Understanding our brain connection to stories.

The short explanation is that our instinct for stories is a survival skill.

For 150 000 years, before writing existed, storytelling dominated human interaction and communication. Through evolution, humans have been rewired and hardwired to think in stories. We make sense of the world through stories. What blew my mind is that scientists discovered that the wiring in our brains turns incoming information into story form BEFORE it reaches our conscious mind. Your brain takes the available information and automatically fills the gaps to make sense of the data. This process is called the predictive mind.[6]

The primary function of your brain is to make sense of information. It is ultimately a pattern-making machine.

If you do not have all the data or information, your brain fills the gaps automatically without you even realising it. In this sense-making process, we often change what we hear to understand the context better. We make assumptions, create new stories, ignore some parts, make connections that might not be there, and misinterpret.

We rarely get the exact version of the story that the person conveying the message intended. Our brain distorts incoming information to help us make sense of it. We become the best fictional screenplay writers ever!

WOW. Stop right there. Take a moment to think this through. No wonder there are so many disagreements and miscommunication!

---

[6] Ayan, S., 2018. *The Brain's Autopilot Mechanism Steers Consciousness.* [online] Scientific American. Available at: <https://www.scientificamerican.com/article/the-brains-autopilot-mechanism-steers-consciousness/>.

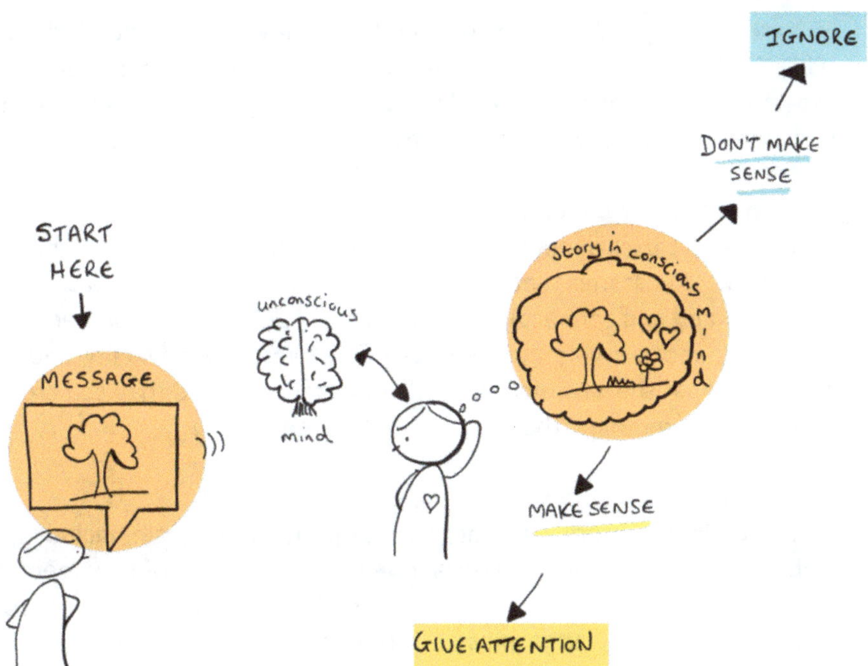

How we make sense of information.

What our brains are looking for?

Like a good recipe, good stories usually have ingredients. Think about the last movie you watched. There is usually a hero or heroine in these stories, some conflict or problem, dragons to slay, adventure or some risk and danger, and an end goal, treasure, or gold. Oh, and don't forget the villain to add some excitement or a twist to a love story.

Our brains try to make sense of all incoming information. If there are gaps in the information offered, our brains assume some of these elements or create their own version to make sense of it.

***

I was so intrigued by all of this that I interviewed Dr. Colleen Lightbody[7] (PhD; MPhil; PCC; PGCNL – Business Owner; Trainer; Coach; Speaker), an expert in neuroscience who explained it in more detail. I asked her these questions and this is what I learned from her:

Stories become pictures.
The visual cortex in our brain takes up more space than the rational part. This means that stories that create images and metaphors are easier for us to understand and connect with emotionally. For example, if someone tells us a story about a young girl's struggle to overcome adversity and adds details of what she saw, heard, smelled, tasted, and felt, they can create a vivid image in our mind that we can relate to personally.

Stories evoke emotion.
These kinds of stories activate various parts of our brain, including the limbic system, which plays a crucial role in the formation of new memories related to personal experiences and emotions. Sharing stories helps us connect and form relationships with others, which is what our brains are wired for. By engaging in social and emotional connections, we build trust and understanding with each other.

Our brains wired for negativity.
Our brains are wired to be on the lookout for potential threats. This is because fear is a natural part of our brain's constant alertness, which is always scanning our environment for anything that could go wrong. In fact, research shows that we are scanning our environment five times per second to protect ourselves from any possible danger. We tend to live in either the past or the future, and fear tends to reside in the future narrative state.

The power of choice.
It's fascinating to consider Viktor E. Frankl's words on the power of choice in the face of fear. He wisely noted that there is a space between stimulus and response, where we have the ability to choose our response, and it is in our response that our growth and freedom lie. To overcome fear, we must first recognise it as a narrative and pause before reacting with the typical fight, flight, or freeze response. It's important to keep in mind that fear is only an illusion, a story we tell ourselves about an anticipated future state.

---

[7] Lightbody, C., 2020. *Are we wired for stories.*

Of course, it's not to say that we shouldn't be mindful of the future or plan for it. However, we often tend to do so in a negatively focused way due to our survival instincts. Our past narrative is often full of self-doubt and negative beliefs, while the future brings uncertainty and thus, fear.

Understanding patterns.

Our brains are exceptional at forming patterns, which helps us conserve cognitive resources and feel comfortable. However, this tendency also means that we may overlook important information if it doesn't fit our established patterns. Uncertainty and the inability to form patterns can produce fear, as we feel out of control. The COVID-19 pandemic was a prime example of uncertainty and fear. During a pandemic, no one knows how it will play out, and that is why people found themselves in a state of fear.

Rewrite internal stories and narratives.

It's important to keep in mind that the stories we tell ourselves hold a lot of power. These stories are shaped by our experiences and become deeply ingrained in our minds over time. It's crucial to become aware of these narratives and to understand them. By doing so, we can begin to step outside of them and create new, more positive stories. This takes conscious effort and attention, and it's important to stay present and mindful in order to recognise when we fall back into old patterns.

Create a happy brain.

Whatever you focus on, whether negative or positive, that is what you are going to create. Any negative emotion creates a physical contraction. When we are scared, afraid, or angry, we go into tight muscles, as opposed to positive emotions that create expansion, an openness and willingness. What we focus on becomes our reality and changes us physically as well.

Our brain and multitasking.

Cognitively speaking, you can do an unconscious task and a conscious task at the same time, but you can't do two conscious tasks at the same time. You can swap between tasks but can't do two tasks concurrently.

* * *

I found my conversation with Colleen so insightful and even baffling at times. Our brains are such a powerful tool and instrument. We've now had time to look at the impact of stories, the interpretation thereof and the role our brain plays during storytelling. But why is it essential to understand all of this?

To be better communicators and connect, we need to create stories that are heard and understood. Please don't leave it up to interpretation. Check in with each other. Connect.

It is even more critical when we use technology to communicate. Think about how often we misinterpret WhatsApp messages. WhatsApp messages and emails do not give the complete picture and context, so be especially careful with these channels. When communicating remember the 7 38 55 rule. People listen to 7% of what is said, 38% percent of the tone of voice and 55% body language.

It is also vital to check in with yourself about the stories you make up about yourself and others. Test these stories and assumptions you are making. Be curious. Challenge assumptions – those things you accept as the truth without clear proof.[8]

Be mindful and aware of your own biases. And if needs be, change or rewrite these stories that keep you from moving forward or connecting with yourself and others.

The recipe of clarity in storytelling.

Step 1: Ask clarifying questions.

In the army and navy, instructions are repeated to ensure they are heard and understood. I am not saying that we should repeat every instruction or message - people would get super irritated with you but be mindful of clarifying if you have an ounce of doubt.

Step 2: Test assumptions.

When you expect something from someone, don't assume that the picture you have in your head is the same as theirs. It most probably is not. To illustrate this, I want you to think about the best hamburger in the world. What does it look like? What is on your hamburger? Is it chicken, beef, or a veggie burger? What extras did you add to yours? Sauces? Now, if we all shared our interpretation of the best hamburger, not one hamburger would be precisely the same. We all know what a

---

[8] 2022. [online] Available at:
<https://dictionary.cambridge.org/dictionary/english/assumption>.

hamburger is, but my hamburger and yours will never look or taste the same unless I share specific details with you.

Step 3: Communicate the picture in your head.

Make sure you clearly communicate the picture in your head with others – at home and at work. This ensures that everyone is clear about expectations and agreements, limiting misinterpretation. For example, when I ask my kids to clean the kitchen, I assume they understand that it means they need to take the clean crockery and cutlery out of the dishwashing machine and pack it away. I also assume that they will fill the machine again with dirty cutlery and crockery and, if I am lucky, wipe off the kitchen surfaces. Does this ever happen? No! Is it their fault? No! Is it my responsibility to be clear? Yes!

It is not your story.

My biggest lesson in life is that we all have stories. We judge people based on our stories about ourselves and them. Conflict usually happens in the space where my story - my reality, which I know as the only truth and your story - your reality, which you may well defend like your life depends on it, collide. When we make space for each other's stories through curiosity, we make space for authentic connection. When we fight to defend our point of view, we cannot listen and be curious to discover why the other person is so passionate about protecting theirs.

You need to realise that you can only own your own story. When my friend asks me for advice, my standard response, which she hates, by the way, is – 'it is not your story!'. We attract other people's stories and make them about us, and in most cases, it is not about us. When something happens or someone says something, we instantly try to make sense of it or fill the gap, and we usually, or mostly, go for the negative version as this is our default state. Remember that as a survival instinct, our brains are wired to look out for anything that could potentially go wrong or harm us to protect us from real or perceived threats. But if we know this is happening, we can consciously challenge the default state and test it. We influence each other's stories, but it is essential to realise that we only own our own stories. And our perspective is not the only perspective – even if we believe it is!

Our stories collide sometimes.

How to bridge the gap.

Let me try and explain a point of view or interpretation of our truths like this. If I blindfolded three kids and asked them to each touch different parts of the same tree —one touches the leaves, one feels the bark, and one feels the fruit it bears — each will have a different experience and perspective of the same tree based on their point of departure or view, right? However, all three will be correct and wrong in their interpretation of this tree.

When we have conflict or a misunderstanding with someone it usually is when our different perspectives or stories collide with one another.

Recipe for understanding strain in relationships.

1.   First, be mindful of the fact that you own only your story.
2.   We need to be aware and mindful of our internal stories. The stories we make up about ourselves, others, situations, and the world around us. Be curious and challenge those stories. Is it accurate? Is it reasonable? Is it generous to give people the benefit of the doubt?
3.   Check in with yourself about your intent – do you want to be right - soothe your ego, or do you want to be in connection with the person?
4.   Is the relationship important enough to invest time into and build a bridge, or are you ready to walk away from the relationship and let it go? Suppose you decide to build a connection; you need to do this from a place of curiosity and kindness. Be curious to understand and be willing to listen and connect. Be present.

Recipe for building a bridge.

1.   No baggage allowed - leave the past in the past and be fully present.
2.   Take only your ID card - the essence of who you are – your values and character.
3.   Stamp their passport - acknowledge the person's experiences, emotions, and map of the world.
4.   Walk over the bridge to meet someone where they are at whether you agree with them or not – it is not about being right or wrong. Be curious to learn about their world and share a piece of your heart with them in turn.

Meet people where they are at, inspired by Hedy Schleifer's TED Talk
The Power of Connection.[9]

The best tool in your toolbox is to pause before you react.
Pause.
Take a breath.
Remind yourself that you own only your own story.
Be curious about other people and their stories.
Stories are wonderful. If we understand our stories, it can be a
superpower.

Own, write or rewrite yours!

* * *

---

[9] 2010. *The power of connection.* [video] Available at:
<https://www.youtube.com/watch?v=HEaERAnIqsY>.

Me Time.

It is now time to reflect. Find some questions to answer, allowing you to discover more about yourself and the stories that drive your thinking and behaviour. We all have stories and make assumptions based on them. To become aware of this, is the first step to connecting better with ourselves and others.

Use the templates on the next page to make notes and add additional notes in your journal should you need more thinking and writing space.

Reflect on the following and complete the worksheets.
My internal stories about me:

1. List three negative stories I tell myself about myself that I would like to change.

2. Flip the negatives into positives, i.e., if you said, "I am not enough", it becomes, "I am doing the best I can", for example. It is important to flip it into something that you can believe!

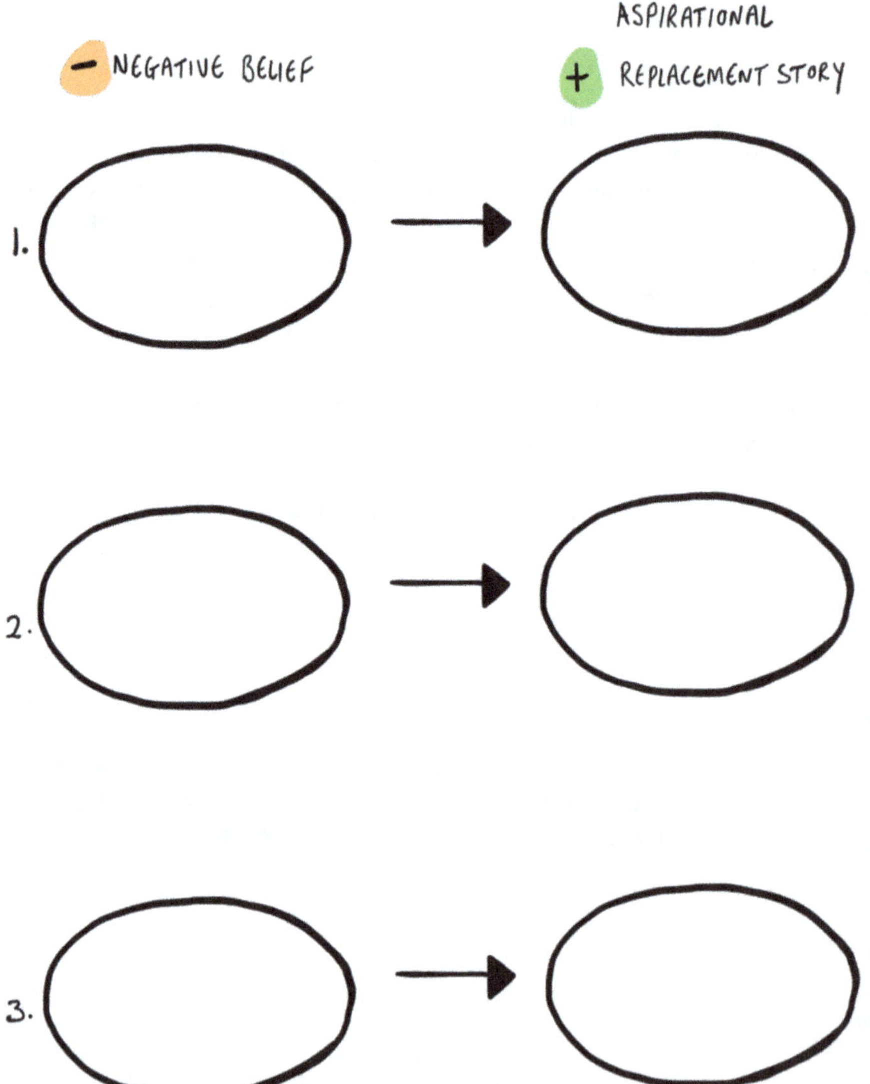

NEGATIVE BELIEF
ASPIRATIONAL REPLACEMENT STORY
1.
2.
3.

My internal stories about others:

1. Identify someone whom you would like to be in connection with. Someone you had a disagreement or an argument with or struggle to connect with.

2. Why is it important for me to connect with them?

3. What are some of the limiting assumptions about them or the situation?

4. What is one thing I can do to build a bridge between me and them?

5. Schedule it: put down a date here and then schedule it in your calendar right now. Act and build that bridge!

I WANT TO BE IN CONNECTION WITH...
NAME

WHY ???

MY LIMITING ASSUMPTIONS
ACTIONS TO BUILD CONNECTION

CHAPTER 3.

TIME TO SHARE BADGES OF HONOUR.

When I was three years old, I got very sick. I first complained about my leg being sore. Not long after this, my family took me to the hospital with double pneumonia and yellow fever. My grandfather, bless his soul, asked the doctors to look at my leg, and specifically my hip, as I complained of it being sore. When they took X-rays, they discovered that something was terribly wrong. The doctors were stumped. They had never seen anything like this. They did not know what was wrong or what to do.

I was getting sicker by the day. A new doctor came to see me a couple of days later and after one look at me and my medical chart, he told my parents that he had to operate immediately. It seemed that I had a rare germ in my left hip which was creating havoc and had even started to spread to my right ankle.

He cut away the bad parts and I stayed in the Intensive Care Unit (ICU) with an extensive gaping open wound in my hip. I remember my dad telling me much later that he had to drive to go and collect specific antibiotics that they administered directly into the wound and that if they gave me too little, the germ would return, and I would die; and if they gave me too much, I could also die. I've often wondered how my parents coped during this scary time. I can only imagine how devastating it must have been to feel so helpless and unsure about seeing your baby girl fighting for her life. Now, we know that it all started with chickenpox. The germ that forms the skin sores somehow got into my bloodstream.

My mom told me that it was a roller coaster ride. She never permitted herself to feel sadness or frustration. She just went with it. She was juggling looking after me in the hospital and caring for my older brothers who were seven and five years old at the time. Riding this wave that no one imagined possible, the impact on the whole family was immense.

I am amazed by the ability and agility of kids. I can't remember all the bad things that happened. I only recall the good parts. Like being asked to cough by the physiotherapist to clear my lungs and not being able to do so correctly, but how impressed I was when the man in the bed next to me in hospital coughed the most glorious big cough ever. "Wow, that was a good one, Mom!" I also remember two amazing nurses who always entertained me. The one was tall and thin and the other was short and a bit heavier set. They would put a stethoscope in my ears, paint speckles on my toenails and sing a well-known Afrikaans song called "Sproetjies" which loosely translates to Freckles but in an endearing manner.

The song tells the story of a man walking in the park seeing a little girl sitting and crying alone, excluded from play because of her many freckles. In the end, she becomes a beautiful ballerina loved by many. It speaks to the fact that he saw the true beauty in her that she could not see herself and about her longing to be able to see herself through his eyes.

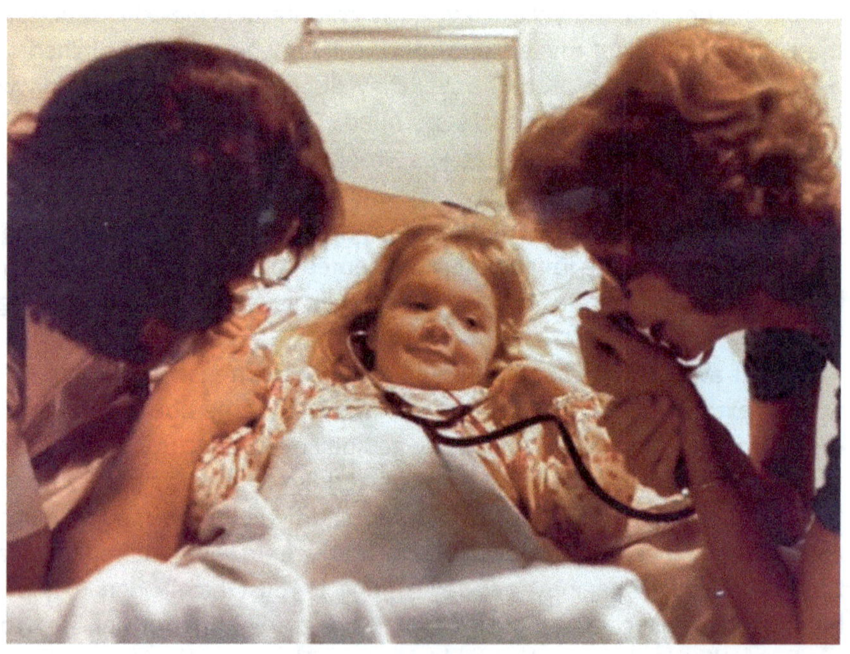

A picture of me in hospital with the nurses singing to me.

When I think about it now, this message of seeing yourself through someone else's eyes is so powerful. Our inner critic sometimes takes over and blinds us to the natural beauty in us that others see, and we can't. There is also a saying that says, "If you spot it, you got it." It means that if you see something beautiful or sometimes also the negative traits, in others, you most probably have the same characteristics. Both negative and positive.

I digress. Back to the story!

I also remember how my dad came to collect me from the hospital after being away from home for a long time. I was the first to ride in our brand-new white Peugeot family car. A proud moment that my dad got to share with me. Everyone waited to welcome me with open arms. I don't remember the hardship at all. I only remember the love and joy.

I spent many months recovering. First in a full-body cast and then walking with special braces – almost like Forrest Gump – remember that movie?

I rocked those braces! I ran as if nothing was wrong. I played swing ball. I was carefree.

In Grade 5, I had my next big operation, followed by a full-body cast. I had to learn to walk again after six weeks of lying down and I can still remember how scared I was to stand upright - it felt very high after lying in bed for so long!. To protect my hip, I had to practice walking in our swimming pool, where I was weightless. Walking is such a simple and basic thing that we take for granted, isn't it?

In Grade 7, I had an operation on my right knee to stop my growth as my left leg was about 3,5 cm shorter than the healthy leg. The medical profession is fantastic. They took an X-ray of my left hand to look at my bone structure to figure out how much I would still grow. Yes, they can calculate it with incredible accuracy! I got about 1.5 cm back in length and was now only 2 cm shorter on the one side, which sounds minor, but it made a huge difference.

I soon appreciated the little things in life like walking and running and moving without pain. I navigated most of my life with joy, happiness, and lots of laughter. But self-pity did sometimes lift its ugly head especially as a teenager and I started to wonder who would ever look at a girl like me. I had moments where I felt broken. Ugly. Not worthy.

What if I never found a boyfriend or someone to love? Who would even consider loving me – the girl with the scars who walks funny?

And when I least expected it, love found me.

Unaware. Unexpectedly. Out of the blue. My love snuck up on me when I was 18, just finished with Matric, and he has never left my side since – loving me for me and nothing else. We got married after a courtship of five years. We travelled the world, had many adventures, and settled down in Cape Town.

After carrying two baby boys, my hip started to create havoc again. I was in real pain and could not even go to the store without taking a painkiller on my return home. I always knew the day would come when I would need to have a hip replacement. Still, I figured it was better to postpone it for as long as possible so that the medical technology could be so advanced that I would only need one more operation in the future. See, hip replacements only lasted around ten years in the past, but with the advancement of technology and medical knowledge, it has changed to a lifespan of 20–30 years. Did I mention that I hate hospitals and needles? The smell of the hospital takes me back to being a three-year-old instantly.

When I turned 35, I made the hard choice to get a total hip replacement. I'm not going to lie – I was scared – really scared! I was worried that the germ was still lying dormant, and that any disturbance could mean that it would return. I was a young mom of two lively boys - five and three years old and my recovery would be a long one. But I knew I had support and love, and I had to push through. I could no longer delay.

I had to go to the hospital the day before the operation and, because we were all worried about the germ making a comeback, I was given a strong antibiotic 24 hours before the time. That day I cried more than I have ever cried in my entire life. I started to cry from the first doctor's visit - an internist, who asked me many questions, but gave up halfway through as I could not stop crying. I cried continuously throughout the doctor visits that day. The poor anaesthesiologist, the physiotherapist, the surgeon, and the nurse had to face the rivers of tears I cried that day. My husband, Theo, sat through all the tears with no judgement or words, just holding my hand with love – the greatest gift he could ever have given me.

I realise now that I was not crying because I was scared. I was mourning the past 32 years. All the heartaches, the struggles, the victories, the defeats. The pain, sorrow, and grief. I was also saying goodbye to an old friend who supported me and did the best it could, even in dire circumstances. A final goodbye and thank you to my mushroom-looking malformed and damaged old hip – release of the past before I could even start thinking of a new future.

On the day of the operation, I was ready. I felt light. I felt excited and a bit scared. The anaesthesiologist looked and sounded like a cool surfer dude with his curly black locks of hair. He was kind and gentle and gave me an epidural like a rock star.

The operation went beautifully. The pain management was excellent - especially the morphine shots. The placement of the new hip meant that my leg was no longer 2 cm shorter, and I could walk normally for the first time in 32 years after the first operation I had had when I was three. It is now ten years later, and I can do most things others can do. I even started to run and ran my first 10 km past the same hospital I had the operation at – something I never thought I would be able to do. I think my love for running is different from most. Every time I run without pain it reminds me of how far I've come and to continue to be grateful and celebrate life.

I am telling you my story as a reminder that we all have battle scars. Some are visible and some are not. I used to hide my scars. By shifting my focus and perspective, I look at the same scars from a different state of mind. My scars are no longer scars but badges of honour. After long contemplation, I decided to celebrate my badges of honour and got this tattoo that symbolises 'perfectly imperfect.'

Perfectly imperfect.

It has been a long, challenging journey. But I am thankful for it as it made me the person I am today. I have more empathy and connection because of it. I have more joy and happiness as life was almost taken from me. The gift I got that I can see with clarity is that I experience life through a different lens. I see the good. I see the sadness. I see the joy. And I choose to see beauty. What a gift! Life did not happen to me. Life happened for me.

Maybe in sharing my badge of honour with you, you may find the strength to look for or even accept yours, mental or physical. By sharing our stories, we give ourselves and others permission to be. Just that. Be you. Scars and all.

Take the time for yourself. Uncover your true essence; show up fully. By doing this, you will not just live, but by living fully, you will have an impact that will make the world a better place. Choose to see your scars as your most significant gifts in life.

* * *

Me Time.

It is now time to reflect. Like before, look at the questions and see what comes up for you. You may experience different emotions while doing this exercise. Be kind to yourself. Have courage and even if you feel a bit uncomfortable, be brave and push through so that you can see and even experience the gifts your scars may offer you.

Use the template on the next page to make notes and add additional notes in your journal should you need more thinking and writing space.

Reflect on these questions and complete the worksheet.

1. What scars - physical or emotional will I be able to turn into badges of honour?

2. What gifts do my scars offer me?

3. What lessons can I take from them?

4. Is there anything I can do to celebrate my scars and turn them into
    badges of honour?

SCARS	GIFTS	LIFE LESSONS

CHAPTER 4.

TIME TO UNCOVER WHAT GIVES YOU JOY.

How to be happy through mindfulness.

One way to train your brain is through something called mindfulness or meditation. This is an in-the-moment focused exercise for your brain. If you think about it, our brains never stop working, even when we are asleep. So, it is important to sometimes pause and still our minds so that we are able to focus on what is important or be present in the moment. We can do this through the practice of meditation or mindfulness. The practice usually includes some focused breathing, and this helps in the process to still our mind and to focus on something specific like gratitude for instance. Mindfulness is a way to still your brain from all the busyness and to be in the moment – 'observing' your thoughts and feelings with curiosity and without judgement as if you are looking at them from the outside as a third party. The beauty of meditation is that the practice is to try, fail, and try again. The process of failing and starting again is precisely the bit that makes your brain stronger and better – building that left frontal cortex and rewiring your brain.

I've been following a very interesting guy by the name of Master Stephen Co. Check out his meditations on YOUTUBE to become a better meditator https://www.youtube.com/@masterstephenco.

He explains that when we meditate, we use our will when we focus on our breath. We concentrate on our breath and project our own will by breathing in and out. In between the breaths, there is a space for awareness where we are open to receive. He uses the example of going to a restaurant with a friend. During the conversation you may sometimes speak and sometimes listen. The same applies to meditation. You breathe and then you receive whatever it is that you need in that specific moment.

Roco Belic, who made the documentary on happiness, refers to a specific gratitude meditation process done by Buddhist Monks that he and his crew tested. *What I Learned While Making a Movie About Happiness, 2013*.[10] In this meditation, you meditate for 20 minutes and focus on yourself, then you focus for 20 minutes on someone you love, then someone you don't know and lastly, you focus and send good thoughts to someone you truly despise. The interesting thing about this meditation is that the more you practice it, the more your brain will grow in that specific area. The frontal cortex lights up with gratitude meditation, and brain scanners can pick it up.

Advice for trying out meditation.

For those who have never meditated, start with 2–5 minutes and work your way up! Also, using a mantra with your breathing. I recently started using a mantra that I love to use – BE on the inbreathe and STILL on the outbreath, is a way to anchor yourself, seeing as our minds run a million miles an hour, and this method helps me to calm down.

The power of gratitude.

Scientists discovered that the left frontal cortex of your brain is your happiness centre[11]. It lights up when you are happy, and scientists can measure the brain activity here. You can train your brain to be happier. And if you exercise this part of the brain, it can grow. Almost like building muscles at the gym with weights. The fact that your brain can grow with a gratitude meditation intrigued me so much that I had to learn more about the power of gratitude. I saw something called the Gratitude Experiment. *An*

---

[10] What I Learned While Making a Movie About Happiness, 2013. *What I Learned While Making a Movie About Happiness*. [video] Available at: <https://www.youtube.com/watch?v=sM_xtk8aqh0>.

[11] Conklin, D., 2013. *The Role of the Brain in Happiness*. [online] Psychology Today. Available at: <https://www.psychologytoday.com/us/blog/in-the-face-adversity/201302/the-role- the-brain-in-happiness>.

Experiment in Gratitude | The Science of Happiness, 2013[12] where they asked a group of people to come in for an experiment. They measured their brain activity before the exercise and again afterward. They then asked the people to think of someone they were genuinely grateful for and instructed them to write a letter to them. Once done, they asked them to call the person and read the letter to them. It was beautiful to watch. But the most exciting part was that the most unhappy people had the most significant spike in activity of the happiness part of the brain when measured again after the exercise. By giving gratitude, you can make yourself happier. My mom always said that it is better to give a gift to someone than receive one, and it is true. Yes, the receiver was also happy, but the giver potentially more so.

Laughter is the best medicine.

Four years ago, my colleague asked me to join her on a two-day course. I said yes! I always do to the things that will stretch me and help me grow. When we got there, she told me that we were going to become laughter yoga leaders. My first thought was that this was crazy, and I felt uncomfortable. Most people there were living an extremely healthy lifestyle, wore the right yoga pants and to be honest, I felt really out of place. I, however, pushed through and embraced the discomfort for two full days of laughter – (ho ho hahaha).

What I found was that laughter is our best tool for happiness.

Let me tell you what I've learned!

Laughter Yoga is a real thing. It was started by a medical doctor in India called Dr. Madan Kataria.[13]

He came across various scientific studies that connected laughter to mental and physical wellness and its benefits. Remember Patch Adams – the movie starring the late Robin Williams who made the kids laugh in the hospital to help them get better? Laughter lowers your blood pressure and stabilises your blood sugar levels. It boosts your immune system and releases all the feel-good hormones like dopamine, endorphins, and

---

[12] 2013. An Experiment in Gratitude | The Science of Happiness. [video] Available at: <https://www.youtube.com/watch?v=oHv6vTKD6lg>.

[13] Laughteryoga.org. 2021. *Laughter Yoga International - Health, Happiness and World Peace.* [online] Available at: <https://laughteryoga.org>.

serotonin to give you a natural high. It releases stress and tension and can even make you look and feel younger.

Dr. Kataria and his wife then decided that it should be put into practice, so they went to their local park in Mumbai with a couple of friends and started telling jokes. They attracted a lot of attention, and the group grew. But alas, the jokes ran dry, and they had to go back to the drawing board to find a way to make this more sustainable.

He then thought that the research also stated that your body does not know the difference between fake and real laughter. And fake laughter releases the same feel-good hormones and good things that happen to your body. He then came up with laughter exercises like any class you would attend at the gym, like spinning class or Pilates routines. He combined it with some deep breathing exercises, the yoga part in laughter yoga.

Lung capacity determines longevity.

Do you know that our lung capacity is about 6 litres,[14] but most of us have shallow breathing and do not use the full capacity of our lungs? Laughter yoga expands your lung capacity.

There are thousands of laughter yoga clubs around the world today and I can tell you that when you feel down or need a bit of a lift, or you want to work on your well-being, look at laughter yoga – it is both fun and good for you. And the whole family can join in.

What gives you joy?

I used to think I could not draw because of a teacher I had in Grade 7. He instructed us to do a still life sketch of some fruit, a calabash and a pot in our art class, which was mandatory in Secondary School. My illustration did not make the grade. It looked nothing like any fruit. When I walked to the front of the class, held up my picture for him to grade, it was not my proudest moment. He commented that I should probably never go into art as a career, and I felt humiliated and small and worst of all – I believed him.

I also had a similar situation in Grade 11, when a music theory teacher called my mom into school and said that I would never pass the music theory exam. I had played the recorder since I was three and was very good at it.

____

[14] *Lung volumes*. (n.d.). Https://Www.Physio-Pedia.Com/Lung_Volumes. Retrieved 2021, from https://www.physio-pedia.com/Lung_Volumes

To proceed to the next level in the practical, however, one had to write a theory exam which, in all fairness, was based more on multiple-line instruments like the piano than one-line instruments like the recorder. So yes, I struggled to 'play' the harmony bit in my mind, so he had a point. It was harder for me. He could not understand why I struggled, because he played the piano and could not put himself in my shoes. He gave up on me and stopped trying. I got help from my recorder teacher, who took the time to understand my issue and addressed it, and I was able to pass my exams and do pretty well. I proceeded to complete the highest practical exam possible with honours.

Why do I tell you these personal stories? I want you to know that people's opinions about what they think or say impact our view of ourselves. And we believe these stories and it becomes our truth. We start to question our capabilities and then give up before even trying because we don't want to prove them right. But what if we could prove them wrong? What if we did NOT allow others to limit us and steal our joy?

What are some of your limiting assumptions or scars? Those barriers that keep you from moving forward? That keep you away from joy? And by the way – what are you saying to others that may become their barriers in life?

Let's be bridge builders, not barrier builders.

For 35 odd years, I lived with those art scars. I hated playing any games that asked for drawing. The game Pictionary was the worst - my crocodile looked like a donkey. I gave up on myself when it came to drawing and I did not even try. To this day, I still sweat a bit more or have my heart race faster if someone asks me to draw or paint.

When I turned 40, I started to rediscover a couple of things. I began to question if I was such a loser when it came to drawing and I began to play with sketch notes. I loved it so much that I have included some of my sketches in this book even though I know I am no illustrator – positive, not perfect has become my motto.

The beauty of sketch notes is that they are merely placeholders for ideas. And something can look 20 percent like the element you are illustrating to be recognisable. I always had the ability. That is the power of stories we have which then become our reality. It took me 35 years to reignite the spark that was always there but dimmed by someone else's opinion of me.

What are some of your limiting assumptions and stories about yourself?

About others?

About what you can and can't do?

Which areas of your life would you like to rediscover?

And what would your life look like if you started to say a big fat YES to the things that are good for you and NO to the things that are not?

Happiness is a choice.

How you spend your time is a choice.

Who you spend your time with is a choice.

And who you listen to or allow to influence and steal your joy is also a choice.

To rewrite your old stories and create new ones is definitely a choice!

Happiness in action.

I spoke to an expert on happiness. Her name is Rosaria Cirillo Louwman,[15] and she is a certified happiness trainer.

Her curiosity about happiness and what drives happiness got her into this line of work. She grew up in the south of Italy, where there was a feeling of 'life is sacrifice'. She questioned this as she believed that we should aim to be as happy as possible.

In her opinion, there are two levels of happiness. One is pleasure, like going to a restaurant with friends, and the other level is fulfilling happiness. This entails the entire vision of a happy life or being optimistic or hopeful about your future.

Defining happiness.

Rosaria's definition of happiness is: "When what we think, what we say and what we do, what we experience and what we feel, are in harmony."

---

[15] Louwman, R. C. (2021, January 29). Happiness. Personal.

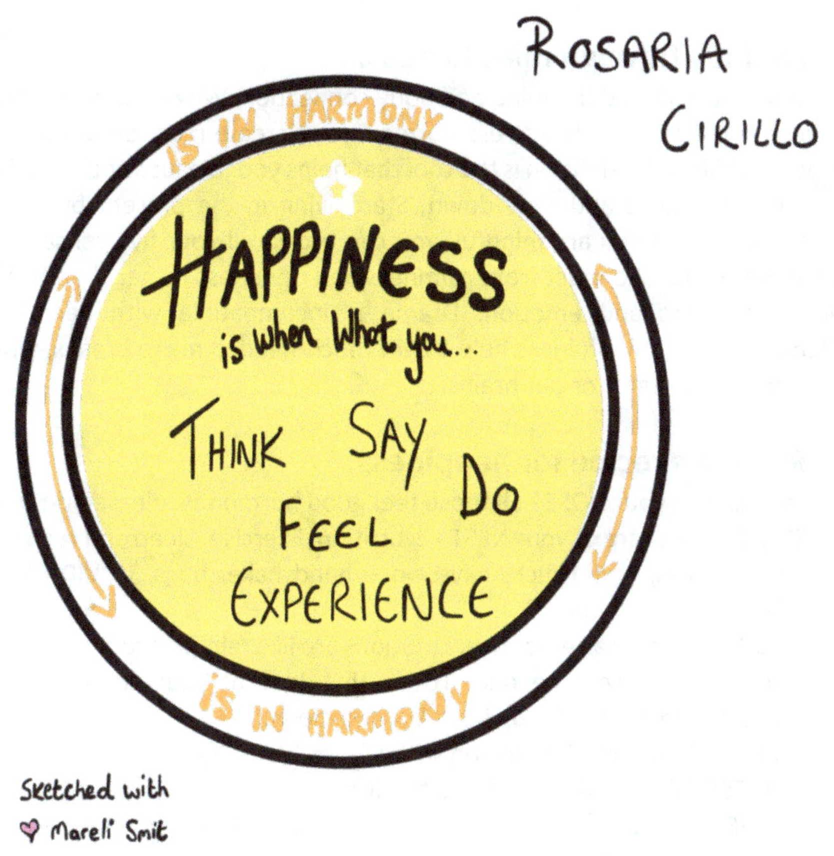

Happiness defined – Rosaria Cirillo

Embodying happiness.

We know that your body can influence your mind, but it also works the other way around. There are five aspects of happiness and one of those is the neuroscience of happiness. When our brains release one or more of the neurochemicals, or as Rosario calls it – DOSE – which stands for Dopamine, Oxytocin, Serotonin and Endorphin – it makes us feel good. You can also trigger those chemicals, especially serotonin. You can produce this by simply remembering happy memories. When you look at an image of a beach, your brain does not know the difference between you being at the beach or just seeing a picture of the beach. When you then activate your five senses and imagine that you smell the beach, hear the sounds of the beach, see it and 'feel' the sand beneath your feet, you can trick your brain into thinking that you really are at the beach. You can thus trigger the feel-good chemicals you need for happiness.

Find joy through mindfulness.

We've mentioned the mind and body connection. We can calm the brain to lessen the cortisol, the stress hormone and create more serotonin, the mood stabiliser. Meditation is the tool that helps you to pause and rest. Take the time to pause and slow down. Start living in the present by paying attention. When you are mindful, you can access all your five senses. You have more space to react from calmness and openness rather than from a place of stress and emotion. Drama is incompatible with happiness. Meditation and mindfulness help us get much-needed micro breaks, which are super important for our brains.

Rosaria's recipe for happiness.

Step 1: Get your DOSE - all those feel-good hormones released on track.
Step 2: Take care of your NEST – Nutrition, Exercise, Sleep and recovery, micro-breaks, and Touch, oxytocin – handshake, hugs. COVID-19 has influenced this so much!
Step 3: Embrace all emotions. Emotions are like rain. To see the rainbow, you must also see the rain. To do this, look at your emotions with curiosity and ask the following RAIN questions.
1. RECOGNISE what is going on with you
2. ACCEPT the emotion and/or situation.
3. INVESTIGATE why you have this emotional reaction and what triggered it.
4. Be curious about what NEEDS are sitting behind the emotion.

Find joy through play!

What also contributes to your inner happiness is sharing and contributing to someone else's happiness. When we give, we also receive in that giving. So, choose to be a joy spreader.

I attended a presentation about the impact of play on adults. In this talk, Viktor *Byström* from the Human Play Academy, mentions that researchers found that play leads to a secretion of a protein called BDNF, or brain derived neurotropic factor, in the brain during play that leads to brain growth.

What was also interesting is that play not only contributes to brain growth but also resilience and survival. So, next time you feel a bit silly when playing, don't. It is good for you and your brain to have fun and play, but just keep in mind that play is your internal experience of an activity, and we all play differently.

So, the invitation is this. Reclaim your joy. Find it. Own it. Cultivate it. And allow more of it into your life. Play, laugh, be mindful and see the impact on your happiness and how it impacts the people around you.

* * *

Me Time.

It is now time to reflect. We sometimes forget the joys that life has to offer. Take the time to remember what gives you joy, what gets in the way of your happiness and how you can create more joy for yourself and others.

Use the template on the next page to make notes and add additional notes in your journal should you need more thinking and writing space.

Reflect on the following questions and complete the worksheet.

1. What gives me joy?

2. If I had a magic wand and there were no limitations, what are the top three things that I would do in life?

3. Why is this important to me?

4. What is getting in the way of my joy and happiness?

5. What is one action I commit to do to bring more joy and happiness into my life?

6. What is one action I commit to do to add more joy and happiness into someone else's life?

MY JOY RECIPE

Joy Blockers	Joy Sparkers	Actions To Joy

WHAT ARE THE CONSEQUENCES

IF I DON'T ACTIVELY

SEEK JOY???

____

____

____

CHAPTER 5.

TIME TO LEAN INTO FEAR.

I've been privileged to work with and watch people from different backgrounds. Working with groups of people from big corporate companies – from the security officers to the CEO – to sharing ideas and conversations with friends, family and even strangers. What I've realised is that people are actually mostly the same. Yes, they may have different value systems or north stars that drive their behaviour, the choices they make and the barriers they need to overcome; but inherently we are very similar and share many of the same hopes, fears and needs.

I found this a revelation, because if it is as I suspect it is, then we have a chance to stop living in fear and start living a fuller, fear(less) life. My hope is that you will also recognise yourself in this chapter and get to know fear not as the enemy but as a passenger on this journey we call life.

I am no expert on fear other than owning my own fears, so in this chapter, I have had to do extra homework and consult others to try and unravel fear. If we understand it better, then maybe we can embrace it more.

One of my favourite writers who speaks to this is Elizabeth Gilbert (Gilbert, 2016) in her book *Big Magic*,[16] who refers to fear as a companion on life's journey, but not the one in charge of making decisions.

---

[16] Gilbert, E. (2016). Courage: The Road Trip. In *Big magic* (pp. 25–27). essay, Penguin USA.

I also read this poem by Khalil Gibran that really describes the process of fear so profoundly and I wanted to share it with you:

"Fear" by Kahlil Gibran[17]

It is said that before entering the sea a river trembles with fear.

She looks back at the path she has travelled, from the peaks of the mountains, the long winding road crossing forests, and villages.

And in front of her, she sees an ocean so vast, that to enter there seems nothing more than to disappear forever.

But there is no other way. The river cannot go back.

Nobody can go back. To go back is impossible in existence.

The river needs to take the risk of entering the ocean because only then will fear disappear, because that's where the river will know it's not about disappearing into the ocean, but of becoming the ocean.

What is fear?

The Cambridge Dictionary[18] defines fear as:

"An unpleasant emotion or thought that you have when you are frightened or worried by something dangerous, painful, or bad that is happening or might happen."

I also like how Nick Vujicic describes fear as, "False Evidence Appearing Real.[19]"

Fear is not our foe, but our friend.

The role of fear is to protect us when something has the potential to harm us. Even though we have evolved as a species, our primal or reptilian brain, the Amygdala, still works full time. When we feel threatened by a perceived or real threat, the fight, flight or freeze response kicks in and is designed to gear our body to deal with this potential threat.

---

[17] Fear by Kahlil Gibran - Your daily poem. (n.d.). Retrieved April 5, 2022, from http://www.yourdailypoem.com/listpoem.jsp?poem_id=3608

[18] *Fear.* Cambridge Dictionary. (n.d.). Retrieved April 5, 2021, from https://dictionary.cambridge.org/dictionary/english/fear

[19] Vujicic, N. (n.d.). *Nick Vujicic.* Nick Vujicic: Fear is often described as False Evidence Appearing Real, Retrieved April 5, 2021, from https://whatsmyquote.com/quote/fear-is-often-described-as-false-evidence-appearing-real/page/4

Our modern or rational brain, our frontal cortex, is responsible for problem solving, memory, language, judgement, impulse control, and reasoning. Our primal brain is responsible for survival, drive and instinct.

Imagine for a moment that you are walking in the mountains with only a water bottle and a snack, and as you come around the corner, you see a big, scary, wild animal like a lion or a grizzly bear. Your survival instinct will most likely kick in and you will either start to run, attack it, or stand totally still as if paralysed, without any movement. This is your body's way of keeping you safe. You do not have to think about it. It happens in an instant, automatically.

In modern society, the same still applies. When your boss or a client yell at you, your Amygdala or primitive brain kicks in, and you have the same response. You can either scream back, say nothing at all, or run and hide in the bathroom. Your primitive brain overrides your rational brain in that instant. This is also called the fight, flight or freeze mode that I mentioned an earlier chapter. It is an automatic response.

When your primal brain is engaged, your modern brain, the rational brain, is not functioning normally. In fact, it could even switch off to ensure your survival. Remember that this all happens in a split second. And at that moment, you have no control. But if you understand your reaction, realise what is happening, and are mindful of it, you can do something about it when it happens.

A tip I got was that when you realise that your reptile brain has kicked in and you want to get yourself back into your rational brain, you should stop and ask yourself three questions: What's your name?; How old are you?; and What is the date today? By doing this simple exercise, you will be able to pull yourself back into the modern or rational brain instantly.

I also remember the story of a call centre agent who had to answer a call from a hysterical lady who phoned for an ambulance for her husband who was in distress. The agent could not get the lady to calm down, realised what was happening, and asked her if she had a kettle and clean towels. The lady calmed down and said yes. The agent then continued and asked her to boil the kettle, take the clean towels and go outside to wait for the ambulance to show them where to stop so that her husband could get the help he needed. After ending the call, the agent's colleague queried the odd request for hot water and towels, to which the agent replied that it was for the benefit of the hysterical spouse. All he did was push her brain back to the rational side to help her calm down. She felt that she could do something and contribute and did not feel so helpless any longer.

* * *

To get some insights into the psychology of fear, I've asked psychology expert, Dr. Karlien Erasmus (Psychologist, PhD, HPCSA – Couns. Psych) for her thoughts on the subject with questions I was curious about. Here are her insights to my questions below.[20]

The difference between fear, anxiety, and a phobia
Fear is an unpleasant emotion that arises from the belief that something or someone is dangerous or a threat - either realistically or perceived by an individual. Sometimes, people are held back by unrealistic fears. Anxiety, on the other hand, is an emotional reaction to a stressful or fearful situation that can make someone feel out of control. However, anxiety can sometimes serve a purpose in terms of coping. Finally, a phobia is an irrational or extreme fear or aversion to something that most people do not experience as a threat, such as an intense fear of insects.

Where fear comes from.
Similar to how our primal brain kicks in when faced with a threatening situation, some fears are ingrained in us and serve the purpose of protecting us. For example, a fear of falling or getting hurt is there to keep us safe and prevent injury. It's important to recognize the difference between a rational fear and an unrealistic fear, so that we can respond appropriately in a given situation. By understanding our reactions and being mindful of them, we can take control and overcome our fears, allowing us to live our lives more fully.

The biggest fears people have.
1. To feel left out, or to feel that they do not fit or belong to a certain group that a person wants to be part of.
2. That others will not like them and will sometimes not set healthy emotional boundaries and rather please or impress others – many times to their own detriment.
3. The fear of being alone – not having meaningful, loving relationships.

------

[20] Erasmus, K. (2017, September 12). Understanding Fear. Personal.

4. To not be successful. More and more people feel that they need to be successful and efficient in everything they do. People put unrealistic expectations on themselves.

It is normal to have certain fears. Know that the purpose of most fears is to protect or to prevent something harmful from happening. Distinguish between realistic and unrealistic fears and choose not to allow unrealistic fears to take control and pacify you.

To express a fear can be a way of taking emotional control of the fear and not allowing the fear to fester, grow, and jump out as an uncontrollable monster.

How to work with fear.

It can be helpful to figure out the root of your fear by:

Examining the situations or events that may have led to this fear or what might be triggering it.

Putting your fears on paper. This can help give you a sense of control over your fear instead of letting it control you.

If you find that a particular fear is severely impacting your daily life, whether in relationships, work, or other areas, it may be worthwhile to seek the guidance of a trained psychologist. During psychotherapy, a psychologist can help you identify the potential causes of your fear, both past and present. Understanding where your fear comes from can often make a meaningful difference in your personal experience. By looking at the bigger picture and considering your fear in the context of your life as a whole, it may be necessary to address other emotional issues that are indirectly contributing to your fear.

* * *

I decided to ask an expert extreme ice swimmer how he deals with fear. Here are some of his insights on pushing through fear.

Case study: Pushing through fear.

To learn more about overcoming fear I interviewed respected extreme ice swimmer Ryan Stramrood.[21] He was one of the first people to complete a 1-mile swim in the arctic at -1°C. He also holds many records including 115 Robben Island crossings and the fastest time anyone has swum across False Bay in South Africa, beating the previous record by 38 minutes in 2021.

Let me explain ice swimming in more detail as I understand it.

When you swim in such extreme conditions your blood flows to your internal organs to protect them from leaving your extremities, like arms and legs, without much blood. This makes swimming even harder when trying to swim with cold limbs. The cold in the water is also not the main issue, but the warming of the body after the swim presents danger. The warm blood starts to circulate throughout the whole body after the swimmer gets out of the water. This means that the ice-cold blood from the extremities then circulates back to the core, the heart and other vital organs. This cold blood flowing into those life-giving organs can be dangerous and needs to be monitored by a medical professional.

Who better to ask about pushing through fear than Ryan. I asked him to share his own experience with fear:

What is your opinion about fear?

"Fear is simply a powerful natural defence mechanism. It is a condition of mind designed to keep us safe, out of harm's way. Safe from physical harm and pain, but also safe from the emotional pain that comes from failure. All good and well for the survival of the human species, but this defence mechanism also keeps us in our comfort zones and underachieving in all areas of life."

What is your relationship to fear?

"My relationship with fear won't be too different from yours. I experience it daily. But I potentially have a better understanding of how our minds use the emotion of fear to make us believe in our own

---

[21] Stramrood, R. (2017, September 13). Pushing through fear. Personal.

limitations. And once you understand that the limit your mind is implementing is potentially only a defence mechanism, you can question it."

How do you personally overcome fear?
"I'm not sure I will overcome it. Perhaps to some extent. But it's more about the ability to rationalise it, to understand why you are experiencing the fear, and then through training, you learn to manage it better. It's a very powerful, natural emotion and I've built some form of relationship with it."

You place yourself in exactly the position that most people shy away from – why do you do it? Why do you challenge yourself and your body the way you do?
"A common question still without a perfect answer. But very simply, fear governs one to remain in a zone of comfort. It covers all areas of life. It is the chemical reaction your body implements to steer you away from 'uncomfortable' places and I have realised, through accident initially, just how much one learns when forced outside of that comfort zone. And more relevant in reverse, how little one learns when operating within the comfort zone. If you don't try new (and often scary stuff), you will not learn new things (about yourself, your abilities, your limits, your world). When you stop learning new things, you stop growing! And when you stop growing, you'll get knocked over. That's the long answer. The short one is that there is a level of addiction to the adrenalin that comes with intense fear and one can simply not feel as alive as when you conquer something you truly feared."

How do you train your brain to stay calm in fear-driven situations?
"Rational thought, regular exposure to the situation, and an agreement with yourself to steer towards the 'difficult' and not away from it."

What does it feel like to overcome all physical and emotional obstacles you challenge yourself with?
"I wish I did overcome all physical and emotional obstacles, but I don't. What is more important to me is that I try. I get off the proverbial

couch, plan, train, fund, and try. And every time I do that, succeed or fail, I learn. I walk away from it a richer man, and that feels good."

What was the biggest fear you ever overcame and how did you do it?
"Diving into -1°C water in Antarctica, Speedo, goggles, cap only to swim a distance (1 mile) which would put me in the water for arguably longer than a human should be able to survive. I was petrified. But through training, understanding, acceptance of severe pain, belief, vital support, and camaraderie of mates, I overcame the fear element and succeeded."

What advice would you give people to overcome fear?
"Spend a lot of time understanding it. Believe that it is an emotion in your head and a chemical reaction in the body designed to set false limits for you. But also know it is there to keep you safe, a little too safe in many situations. So, if your fear suggests you shouldn't jump into a fire, probably best to listen to it. But if fear suggests you should not try something new in business, relationships, life or sport, you should probably challenge it – and realise that it is you challenging and improving yourself!"

What stood out for me in conversation with both Karlien and Ryan was the fact that leaning into fear is super important. Even if it is scary and uncomfortable!

Ultimately, you have a choice in life and happiness – stagnate or embrace the mess, do the things that frighten you, and be curious about the things blocking you from moving forward.

Step into your power – the more you face your fears, the less power it has over you. Take back the steering wheel of your life. Boogie dance with your fear and redirect that energy.

Recipe for taming fear.

There is no recipe to combat fear, but the first step is to acknowledge when you are in a state of fear and make better choices.

Step 1: Suspend judgement.
Stop being so hard on yourself. Ask yourself – what advice would I have given my best friend? And then speak to yourself in your best friend's voice.
Step 2: Acknowledge the fear.
It is impossible to push the fear down – it will always pop up again in strange and mysterious ways. It can surprise you and show its face as anger, sadness, or negative behaviour. Rather than ignoring fear, embrace it, and find the lesson it is trying to teach you. The harder you push it away, the louder it will scream for attention, like a toddler who throws a tantrum on the floor seeking attention and an audience.
Step 3: Do not fight it but lean into fear.
Even if it is scary and uncomfortable so that you can move through it.

Fear is part of life. Once you accept this and stop fighting it, you can lean into it and live a life not dictated by it.

* * *

Me Time.

It is now time to reflect. Fear is something we all have. We tend to try and steer away and avoid fear but take a moment to look at the fear in your life with curiosity, kindness and care, and see what happens for you.

Use the template on the next page to make notes and add additional notes in your journal should you need more thinking and writing space.

Reflect on these questions and complete the worksheet.

Choose a situation that is currently creating fear in your life – it can be something at work or home.

1. What scares me the most?

2. Why does this scare me?

3. What is the worst that can happen?

4. What if this did not happen? How would I feel?

5. What will happen if I face my fear?

6. What will I deny myself if I don't face it?

MY FEAR	WHY	WORST OUTCOME

How will I
feel if the
worst does
not happen?

What will
happen if
i face my
fear?

what will i
deny me
if i don't
face it?

CHAPTER 6.

TIME TO BE BRAVE.

We have a better understanding of fear and the role it plays in our lives. To move forward in designing the life you desire, you need to up your bravery skills and equip yourself to show up fully and tame those dragons that are keeping you back.

How to combat fear

When we are in a state of fear, it is disempowering. As part of our bravery training, we need to put some ammo into our backpacks.

Our limiting beliefs and perspectives lead to us losing confidence in ourselves and our abilities. We start to question everything and then this state becomes our reality.

This reality leads to anxiety. The feeling of worry, thinking about what can go wrong, and loss of control which, in the end, leads to doubt. And in most cases, when doubt takes over, we step back. We don't even attempt to do anything and become paralysed by our fear.

I believe that the antidote to fear is love, acceptance, gratitude, mindful awareness, acknowledgment, healthy habits, connection, focus, and choice.

When you look at fear with this new lens on, you will react to it differently. When your perception of fear changes, so will you.

Let's imagine that your fears are like dragons. Your first instinct is to either run away or slay the dragon, right? Rather than to go against those instincts of fighting or fleeing from the dragons, let's recognise them, acknowledge them and then tame them. A tamed dragon is much less scary. But taming a dragon does not happen overnight – be patient!

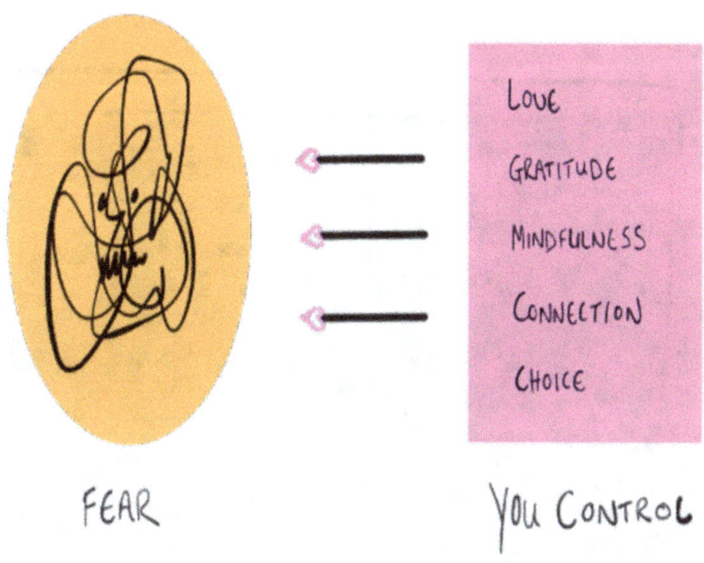

The elements to combat fear.

Assess your blind spots.

We all have blind spots. Blind spots are the areas and aspects of our lives that we may not be aware of, consciously or unconsciously. We tend to ignore these blind spots to avoid the shame we feel when acknowledging our own internal fault lines. Our fault lines are those feelings, thoughts, actions, behaviours, or gaps we all have that we may not be aware of or choose not to see and acknowledge, seeing as they are usually not so positive.

Our beliefs about ourselves and others inform our blind spots. An example of one of my many blind spots is that I avoid difficult conversations as I am a people pleaser and will do anything to avoid conflict. Another one is that I go it alone as I am afraid that if I ask for help, people may think that I am weak. Find out what your blind spots are, be curious and acknowledge them so that you can develop strategies to deal with them more positively.

Can you think of any of your blind spots? And if you can't, ask someone close to you to help you identify them. It may be hard to hear but can be a real gift. Again, I want to remind you that we are all human and far from perfect. It takes bravery to look at your fault lines with curiosity and care, acknowledge them and then choose if you need to address them or not.

Blind spots can teach us about ourselves.

Bravery training recipe.

Getting brave fit takes time and practice. Here is a list of practical exercises to get you where you want to be!

1. Get fear fit. Put in the hours and the hard work. They say it takes 10 000 hours to become an expert in any field, so start practicing bravery right now. I began to say yes more than no to everything that is good for me even the things that took me right out of my comfort zone. See everything that scares you as building your bravery muscle. You may sometimes fall flat on your face, but get up, learn from it, and move forward.

2. Say no with respect. Another thing most people struggle with is boundary setting. To say no respectfully and tell people what is okay or not okay for you is the most significant gift you can give yourself, as it shows respect to you and others. If you keep letting people step over your boundaries, it will lead to resentment. It will make you feel powerless and less worthy. Stop the cycle – be brave and claim back your space.

3. Let go of perfect and go for positive. We don't try because we are afraid to be judged, afraid of failure, or even scared of success in some cases. Live in the moment and don't worry about what happens next. While you worry about what might happen, you may well miss opportunities right in front of you and what a waste that is.

4. Surround yourself with superheroes. The saying is that you are what you eat. But I want to counter that and say you become your conversations and the people you surround yourself with. Read books or listen to audiobooks and talk to people who have overcome adversity and are happy to share their learnings and experiences. I've found that most people are generous. But it is up to you to ask for what you need.

5. Enjoy the ride. What you may find easy to do now initially was hard. Think about the first time you learned to ride a bike; you fell a couple of times before mastering it. Now you are on autopilot and your muscle memory has kicked in. All change is hard at the beginning. It is messy and then becomes beautiful. Progress is not straightforward. It is supposed to be messy because humans are messy and complicated. Accept that your roadmap may consist mainly of dirt roads and not highways. But you can go much higher and reach so many beautiful spots on a dirt road compared to a highway.

Practice pushing through with a brave heart.

Fear may sometimes feel like a dark cave filled with bats, creatures and potential danger.

With courage, bravery, grace and humility as your armour, I invite you to enter your cave with curiosity in the next exercise. It may feel uncomfortable but push through. The bats and spiders you fear in the cave may be protecting the gold you seek.

As with most training, you will have failures and successes. Bravery training will take time, so be patient with yourself while you learn the skills you require to live a life you deserve.

* * *

Me Time.

It is now time to reflect. Fear is something we all have. We tend to try and steer away from and avoid fear but take a moment to look at the fear in your life with curiosity, kindness and care, and see what happens for you.

Use the template on the next page to make notes and add additional notes in your journal should you need more thinking and writing space.

Reflect on these questions and complete the worksheet.

1. What are my blind spots that I am aware of?

2. What do my blind spots teach me about myself?

3. What is the one thing that scares me the most or is keeping
    me back from living the life I desire? What dragon do I need to tame?

4. What is my current belief about what scares me most?

5. Flip the belief to something more positive.

6. What action can I take to tame the dragon from this new/more positive perspective?

TAME THE DRAGON

Name the fear

____

OLD BELIEF	NEW BELIEF

II.

DESIGN YOUR LIFE BLUEPRINT.

Now that you've discovered or rediscovered yourself and what is most important to you in the DISCOVER chapter, it is time for you to DESIGN a blueprint for your life. At the end of this section you will be equipped with all the necessary tools to create the life you desire.

Before we dive in, let's take a moment to assess where we are right now.

Answer the following statements as either true or false. Circle your answer.

1. I know what values drive my behaviour?

True   False

2. I am very aware of the stories, memories and beliefs that keeps me from living my best life.

True   False

3. I prioritise my life goals daily.

True   False

4. I live a very balanced life.

True   False

5. My routine and habits support my goals.

True   False

Let's dive right into the ingredients needed to design a fantastic menu and meal.

CHAPTER 7.

TIME TO VALUE YOUR VALUES.

The first thing you usually see on the walls of big corporate companies are their company value posters or vision and mission statements. And it is mostly along the lines of respect, integrity and trust. Unfortunately, in most cases, the interactions with the companies do not always illustrate or reflect the behaviours that best support those values.

I believe it is imperative to live life by your values. To show up and make sure that what you do and say reflects who you are, showcasing your values to the world through your behaviours. Values should be doing words. If you say integrity, trust and respect, for instance, what are the behaviours that will showcase and support those words?

Sometimes, however, our behaviour may not align with our values, or we say or do something that takes us out of our integrity. It happens. No one is perfect.

I recently had an experience where I said something to a very good friend within a group context, intended as a joke, but it pierced her skin and really hurt her. I was out of integrity regarding my values of kindness and connection. I felt terrible. I had a choice at that moment to let it go and hope that it would resolve itself. But to be in my integrity again, I had to take accountability. Accountability goes beyond saying that you meant well or that it was not your intent to hurt someone. It was like an egg that broke. I broke the egg. I could not really fix it or unbreak it. I could only say that I broke the egg, and I was sorry. I needed to say it, but more importantly, she needed to hear me say it, so that we could be in connection again. There is still a scar, but in time it will heal.

What determines my behaviours, actions, and attitudes are not only my values, but also my beliefs and perspectives, and how I act on those values or beliefs is determined by the state of mind in which I am.

If we understand values, beliefs and mindsets and are more mindful and intentional, we can also recognise and acknowledge the values, beliefs and states of people around us and what drives them - making connection easier.

Let me explain.

We all know what values are. Those things that our parents taught us and that we try to instil in our kids.

Let's say my values are kindness and love, but my state of mind is negative and only focused on the stuff that goes wrong. It will be tough for me to behave in a way that reflects my values. The thing is that my state or mindset is a choice. If you do not choose, the default setting of most people's state will be negative. That is why it is so easy to go down that road. If you remember the discussion I had with Colleen Lightbody, she mentioned that our brains always look for what could go wrong as a survival tactic. If you do not focus on your mindset every day, to choose what state you will be in, the chances are that it will default to the negative. You have a choice about what you will do and who you want to be in your daily life. Choosing your attitude will determine your state of mind. Will you be open and positive and look for the good in people and situations or will you be closed off and negative and have no patience with people around you?

What also plays a role in our behaviours are our beliefs. Beliefs are formed from past experiences or passed down through cultures, our parents, or society. For example, I grew up thinking that it was unacceptable to stand out and be unique and that conforming was the only way to fit in. This belief affected my behaviour. If I did not change this belief, I would continue to make 'normal' or 'no-risk' choices to stay the course. This is but one example.

There are many. One example of a belief people may have, is that they are not good enough. And if you genuinely believe that you are not good enough, this will affect your behaviour, actions, and the choices you make or don't make.

How do we shift beliefs?

To live in your integrity, it is essential to discover your central driving force values. You may subscribe to many values, but we want to uncover your core values. It is also important to look out for and acknowledge the values you see in others if you're going to build strong relationships.

Me Time.

It is now time to reflect. We all know our values, but sometimes, we step out of our integrity when our behaviours do not reflect our values. Let's unpack our values and the behaviours that support them in more detail. Once you know your values and behaviours, try to see if you can spot what values other people value most and connect with them on a different level.

Use the template on the next page to make notes and add additional notes in your journal should you need more thinking and writing space.

Let's get practical.

Recipe: Discover your core values.

Step 1: Write down five values that are most important to you personally.

Step 2: Rate these out of 5 where 1 is the most important and 5 not important.

Step 3: Identify the top two values – thus, values rated #1 and #2.

RATE

RATE

RATE

RATE

RATE

You will now create your own values road map. Here is an example of a complete road map. Use the blank worksheet to create your own values road map. Follow the steps below to complete your own map.

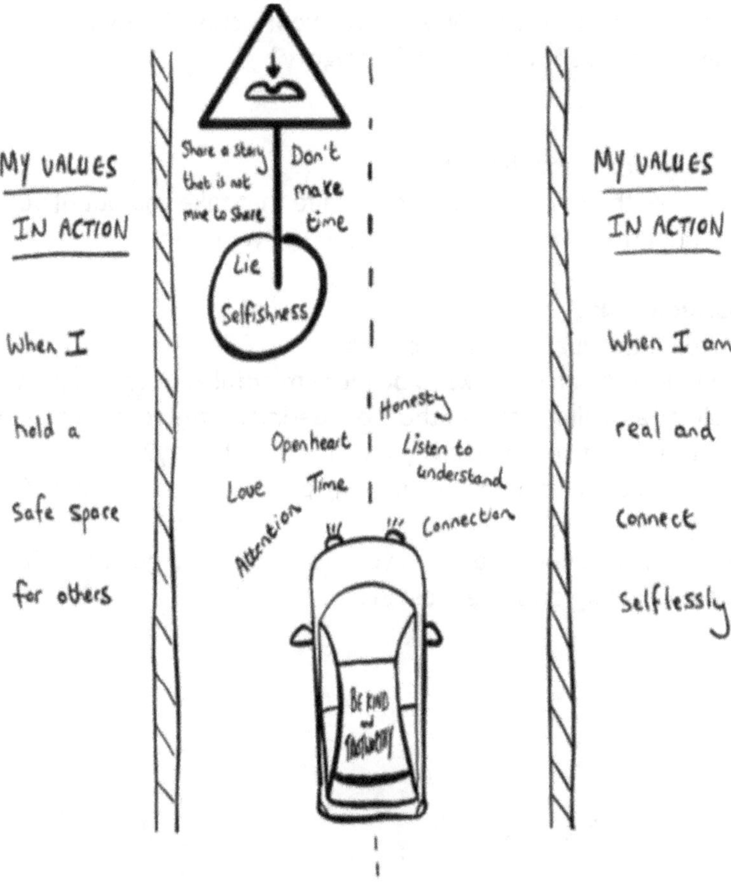

Your guardrails in life.

Instruction 1:
Use the template on the next page for this exercise. Write down your #1 and #2 values from the previous exercise on the roof of the car. But take the value and add a verb to it to make it an action.
For instance, kind becomes *be kind.*

Instruction 2:
On the road in front of the car where the lights are shining.
Write down the behaviours that illustrate and illuminate your values best to the world at home, at work and generally. What lights the way for you? How do you show up? What drives your actions? When are you living your values or showing up with integrity?

Instruction 3:
Write in or around the pothole.
What are the things or situations in life that take you out of your values and integrity? The potholes you need to avoid in life.

Instruction 4:
Write on the guardrails of the road.
What actions can you take to be more mindful about getting on the road again after falling into a pothole or veering off the road – what are the guardrails that keep you going and in your integrity?
It can be people, actions, or anything practical you can think of.

Use the image you created as your road map and guidance system as a reminder of what you value most in life.

My values road map.

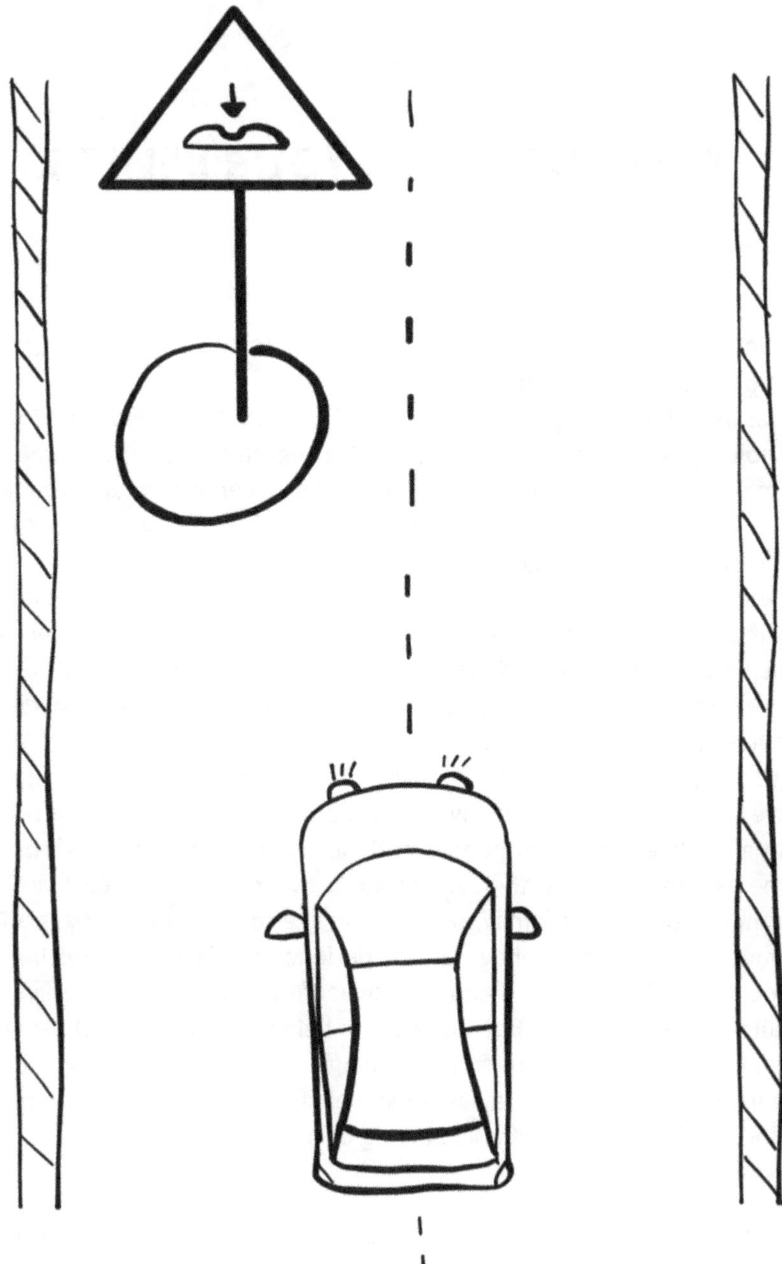

CHAPTER 8.

TIME TO RELOOK YOUR BELIEFS.

Beliefs are defined in the Collins Dictionary as[22] "a feeling of certainty that something exists, is true, or is good."

I was in an Afrikaans primary school, and we only started learning English as a subject in Grade 4. I was terrified of the English teacher. Her name was Ma'am Geertsema, and she used a whole lot of green eyeshadow as make-up on her eyes, and we were only allowed to speak English in her class even if no one could at that stage.

She was very strict, and the rule was that no one could chew chewing gum. If she caught you chewing in her class, you had to throw your bubblegum into a jar and pick another gum from the jar that someone else had chewed on before. I cringe when I think about this now. My kids will never have a story like this to tell their kids one day.

This story reminded me of our beliefs. They are almost like chewing gum, and we sometimes chew our own beliefs and then throw them into a jar potentially influencing other people, and then we take other people's beliefs and chew on them a bit further. All the stories we hear and the feedback we get from our peers, our family, our culture, the media, our teachers affect the way that we think, behave and experience the world. These beliefs, which could be both positive and negative, affect the way that we live our lives and how we show up. But some of the beliefs we have do not serve us. They may even be keeping us from reaching our full potential.

I think it is time to throw away those beliefs that are all chewed up. It is time for new beliefs. Minty fresh. Serving us better.

---

[22] HarperCollins Publishers Ltd. (n.d.). *Belief definition and meaning: Collins English Dictionary*. Belief definition and meaning | Collins English Dictionary. Retrieved April 5, 2022, from https://www.collinsdictionary.com/dictionary/english/belief

Evaluate beliefs with curiosity.

Imagine a donkey tied to a pole with a rope, and the rope has a huge ugly knot in the middle. What would happen to the knot if the donkey walked away from the pole? The knot would become tighter, right? And if the donkey moved closer the pole? Would it be easier for the farmer to untangle the knot?

The same applies to beliefs that stop us from moving forward. If you ignore the beliefs and walk away, the knot will become even tighter, but if you move closer to the knot and become curious about it, the chances are that you will be able to untie and get rid of the knot, and it may even bring you closer to yourself and others. An alternative but more permanent option is to cut the rope representing your old limiting beliefs. What I do like about untying rather than cutting the knot is that it allows you to inspect the belief more closely with curiosity to understand it better and then you can decide if you want to hang onto the belief or instead get rid of it. There is symbolic learning and growing in this process for me. What happens when we hold onto our limiting beliefs about ourselves is that we get in our own way to move forward. And if we have limiting beliefs or assumptions about others, it is difficult to grow a connection.

Why stick with something holding you back when you can use this knowledge and experience to catapult yourself and your relationships forward?

Mindset and perspective taking is a choice.

Have you ever heard someone say happiness is a choice? When I heard it the first time, I thought it was nonsense. How can you choose happiness if everything in your life is going wrong? I always believed that happiness is directly attached to what happens to you in life. I also thought that what people say and do will determine your happiness. People make me feel a particular emotion. You can make me happy or sad. Now, I have a different belief, I want to challenge you to open your mind and hear me out. Try this on like a new jacket, test it, and see what you think. I want to argue that no one is so powerful that they can make you feel anything.

True, they can influence your circumstances, and you may have an emotional reaction, we are human after all, but you always have a choice of what you do with the emotion that arises or what you will focus on, or even how long you choose to linger on a specific emotion. The choice you make, however, will be affected by the perspective from which you are making that choice. For instance, when something happens, good or bad, you may have different perspectives. For instance – is this the beginning or the end? Is it a problem or an opportunity? Is it stretching you to be better, or is it breaking you? These different perspectives will drive different behaviours or reactions.

Let that sink in for a moment.

You are not a victim of other people's opinions or actions. You are a competent, creative, resourceful and whole human being that can make choices. Not making a choice, however, is also a choice.

It is easy to blame others and be the victim of their words and deeds, or you can blame life for handing out blows. Yes, life can be challenging, but when you blame others, you are not taking responsibility for designing your life. Sure, you are human and will have emotions and it is human to react or act on those emotions. It is more about getting stuck in emotions and not getting out of the drift sand. Let me give you an example to illustrate. Let's say that I am driving in traffic on the highway into the city. I get stuck in heavy traffic. The taxis and every second car almost push me off the road to jump the queue to get in front of me – we are all late for work or a meeting or wherever we are going. Now I have a choice. I can get irritated, throw a middle finger, swear, cry, complain to everyone I see at work and back at home about these bad drivers. When I do this, I choose to give away my power to strangers. I give them control over not only my day but over my whole day, my energy, and all my actions, interactions, and reactions for the rest of the day. On the other hand, those other drivers did not give me a second thought at all and went on their merry way.

The other choice I have is to acknowledge that I am pissed off, or at least annoyed, then move on and shift my focus to something more positive, like listening to great music or an audiobook. If I let go of the little things, they will not become big things, leaving space for expansion, happiness, and joy.

Recipe for choosing your reaction.
1. Choose your battles.
2. Decide where you will spend your energy.
3. Ask yourself if it is worth it and what you gain or lose in every situation.
4. Make the choice that serves you and the people around you.

In terms of choices, ask yourself what it takes to make choices that align with the life that I say I want to live. Then make choices – big and small that will help you stay in alignment with your goals and values. For instance, if my wellness goal is to be healthy and exercise, I need to choose to put on my running shoes and go for a run rather than sit on the couch and watch TV. If my financial goal is to save enough money to go on a trip at the end of the year, my choices in spending money should stay aligned to that goal. If I say I want to be happy, I will choose the things in life that bring me joy and decide to focus on the positive despite the negatives that life throws my way.

This is no easy task – it is an ongoing process, but so worth the effort!

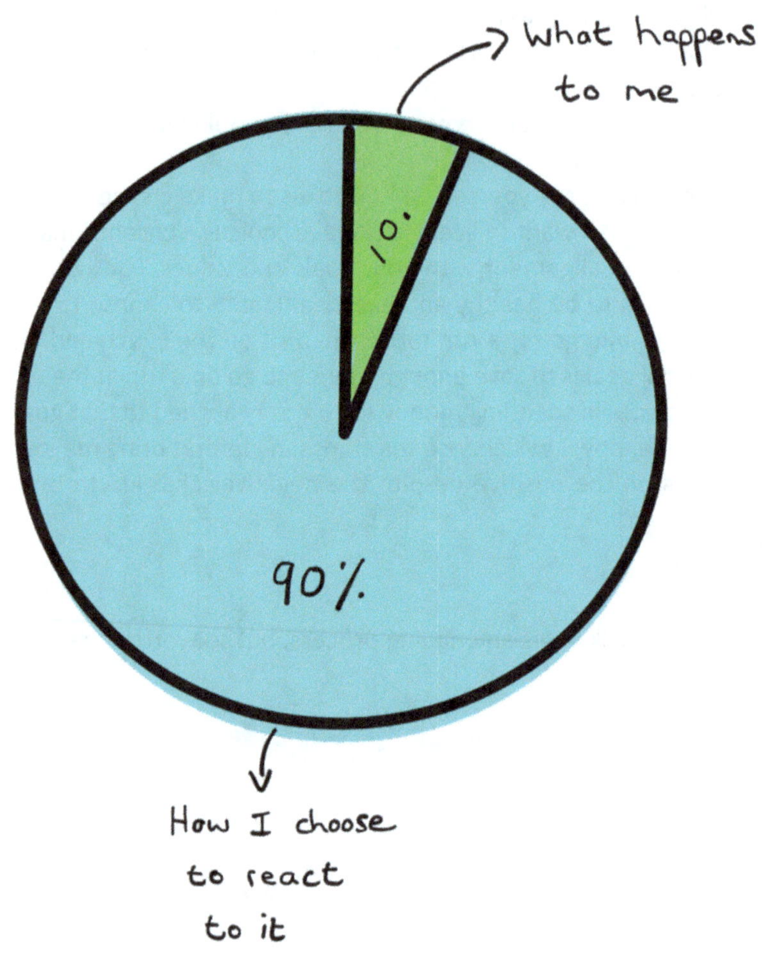

How you experience life is a choice.

* * *

Me Time.

It is now time to reflect. We have many beliefs that have been formed over many years and these form our world view – how we see ourselves and others. This exercise will help you uncover some of your own beliefs and determine whether they are serving you or not.

Use the template on the next page to make notes and add additional notes in your journal should you need more thinking and writing space.

Reflect on the following questions.

1. Write down three limiting beliefs that you currently have about yourself or others, i.e., I do not have the skills, I am not good enough or other people cannot do the job I do as well as I can.

2. Are these beliefs true?

3. Flip your beliefs around to positives, i.e., I have the skills, I am good enough, others can do the job.

4. Choose one new perspective from point 3. What would my life look like if I handled it from this new perspective or fresh belief?

5. What is one thing I can do differently from this new perspective?

6. What impact will this have on me and the people around me?

BELIEF	TRUE	FALSE	POSITIVE BELIEF
1.			
2.			
3.			

ACTION

____

____

____

IMPACT

____

____

____

CHAPTER 9.

TIME TO REBOOT YOUR BRAIN.

Colleen Lightbody speaks about our brain being a pattern-making machine. It likes to connect the dots. It likes predictability. It tricks us into thinking that we do not like change. The thing is that most people are not scared of change itself. What makes them uncomfortable, however, is TO change.

Can you think of anything you do that can qualify as a pattern? Think about the following. Do you always sit in the same spot at university or church? Or do you always park in the same parking area at the shopping centre and enter at the same entrance? Do you look for and connect with a particular type of person at work or social gatherings? I certainly do. It is seamless and easy. It is predictable and safe. It gives me a sense of security. And these are some patterns I can see clearly. It is a default setting that most of us have. I am not saying that it is good or bad. I merely want us to focus on it more intentionally.

Patterns in our life.

Let's look at some of the patterns that do not serve us. What are the habits, the thoughts, the words we use, the beliefs and assumptions we make, and the perceptions or perspectives that distract us from moving forward?

To illustrate this, for instance, let's say that you planned a lovely dinner for friends. You spent a lot of time planning it; you went to the store and bought what you needed to make the evening special. You even got candles and extra special snacks. An hour before the event, your friends WhatsApp you and cancel without explaining. They apologise, but it feels insincere.

Words that come to my mind are disappointment, being mad about the wasted time, money and food.

The default pattern here is that you make it about yourself. You take their story and make it your story. They chose something else or someone else above you. Or they had a crisis and did not feel comfortable sharing it with you. Their choice not to come to your dinner has hugely impacted you. Your internal narrative is anger, but what sits behind it is hurt. They may have strengthened your own belief that you are not good enough.

Was this their intention? Probably not. Did it hurt? Sure. Is it really about you? NO.

You have a couple of choices here. You can acknowledge the emotion of being hurt and disappointed. You can be curious and kind and check in why they cancelled. They probably have a legitimate reason. This allows them to give you a complete picture.

You can choose to stay angry and hurt and make the evening a living hell for your family who have to deal with your bad mood. You may have a long-standing belief that you are not always a great mother. When you are short-tempered with your kids that evening, because you are feeling emotional, it further enforces your belief that you are not a good mother. This then makes you even angrier at your friends who you believe have placed you in this position in the first place. See the vicious circle?

Back to your dinner disappointment...You can choose to still make the evening great by shifting your perspective and choosing a different attitude. You can choose to either do a last-minute invite to good friends and tell them you have too much food that will go to waste or have an intimate dinner with your family and still make it a great.

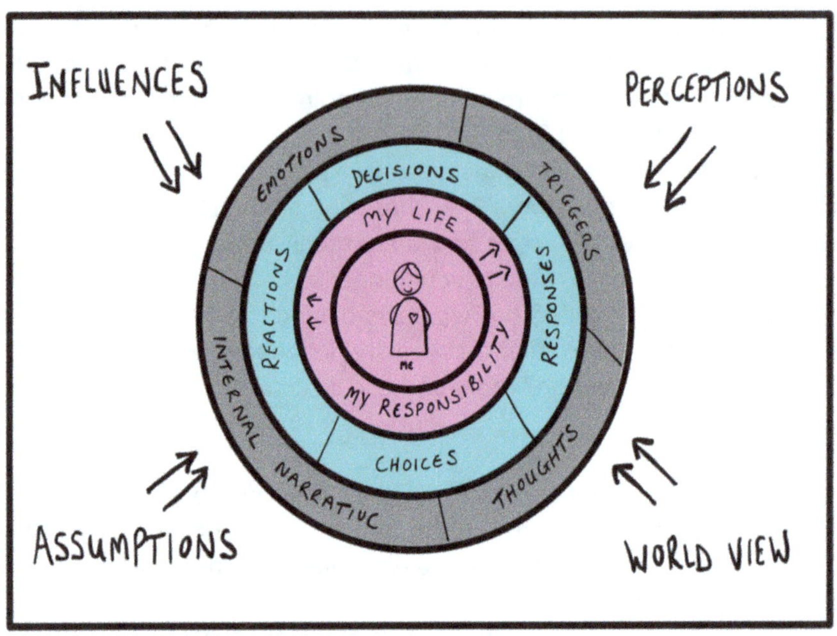

Life deconstructed: Beliefs + Perspectives + Choice = My Reality

Retrain your brain.

It does take effort not to default to your old ways. Making new choices needs to be intentional. It will be tough, BUT once you get the hang of it and become aware of what triggers you, you can start to adjust and retrain your brain. It is so powerful to push the reset button and unlearn years and years of messages, beliefs and habits. Be intentional about your thinking rather than allowing your brain to be lazy and default. Choose different words and actions and this will then become your default. If you continue to focus on your limitations, you will stay caught up in them. You truly can become what you focus on. But it is a choice only you can make.

Upgrade your default settings and be the programmer of your life.

I love technology. I love how I can work on any of my devices, how integrated they are, and how easy and intuitive it is to switch from one device to the next.

When I got ready for one of our online workshops recently, I received that dreadful message informing me that my computer memory was almost full. I Googled, as one does, possible solutions to clear some space. I discovered that the stuff that took up most of my 250GB storage space on my computer were the items in my trash or bin folder. I deleted the bin items and got 50GB back in an instant. This allowed me enough capacity to download the latest upgrade for my laptop. But more importantly – before I deleted the bin items, I ran a backup – saving the most important files so that I could use them as a reference in the future. While I was busy, I also ran a virus protection program on my computer. Those that pick up viruses or trojan horse virus files that penetrate your system and pop up when you least expect them and create havoc and disaster.

All of this triggered a thought: I could not save any new files. I could not run the latest updates, and I could not sync my phone or do backups because my computer memory was low. And why was it low? Because I had too many files and items, holding onto stuff that I did not want or need any longer and that were not serving any purpose.

How true is that for our lives as well? How many things are we holding onto that are not serving us?

There is a solution though.

The downside, however, is that it takes a bit of time to clear our cache. To decide what to keep and what to delete.

The upside is that if we take the time to do this for ourselves, there will be so much more space for expansion.

Make space for expansion.

Think about the following in your life at this moment in time.

1. Are the things I am holding onto serving me?
2. What is preventing me from upgrading my life?
3. What am I filling my hard drive storage with?
4. Is it essential to hold onto a specific belief, thought, idea or fear I have?

5. What are the items in the bin that I forgot were there that I need to uncover as it is taking up unnecessary space?
6. Are those trojan horse viruses – the fears, limiting beliefs or assumptions about myself and others impacting my choices and behaviours, lurking behind the scenes – waiting to unravel my life?
7. Is there anything I am still holding onto that happened in the past that is taking up so much space that I cannot look to the future?

Maybe it is time to take the lessons from the past and then let go. Thank the past you. Create space for the present and future you. Take the time to pause and uncover what you want to hold onto or what to let go of, allowing yourself some space for an upgraded version of you.

Your operating system.

Let's unpack the analogy of computers even further. I am no computer genius, but I know that all computers run on an operating system, like Microsoft Windows, Apple MacOS or Linux. Think of it as the computer's brain coordinating all the hardware and software, ensuring that the computer runs smoothly. Most computers are pre-loaded with a standard operating system, but it is possible to upgrade or even change the operating system entirely if you choose to do so. A computer cannot run without an operating system.

As humans, we also have an operating system which I like to call the unconscious mind. The unconscious mind is our super powerful operating system that runs pre-conditioned programs, our worldview is influenced by our life experiences and conditioning. It is our autopilot setting where things happen without us thinking about it. It helps us connect the dots and to create patterns.

Our conscious mind, however, is the place where you can choose which programs to upload and run on your operating system. Think of it as the apps you choose to load onto your phone or computer to personalise it for yourself. The ultimate goal is synching your unconscious and conscious mind to ensure balance and harmony. It will require mindfulness, choice, reprogramming, time and much more effort until your unconscious mind runs the programs you choose rather than the pre-selected programs of the world.

Version 2.0 of you.

Imagine this version of yourself: Version 2.0, where the corrupted files are fixed. Where you are the programmer of your life. Where you have access to the latest tools and apps. Where you use an operating system of your choice and expand your capabilities. Just imagine! Delete the things that no longer serve you. Watch out for the viruses that may derail you. Reboot your life. Upgrade it to the latest version. Add new positive programs to your operating system and start to believe in the story of YOU!

* * *

Me Time.

It is now time to reflect. We all have things that take up space in our lives. If those things are unnecessary to you, what room does it take up that takes away space for what you want to have? To unpack them, do some work choosing the things you want in your life and making space for them.

Reflect on the following questions.

Think about your own life now.

1.   What is taking up space in my life?

2. What memories, hurt, anger, sadness or stories am I holding onto that prevent me from living my best life?

3. What files (beliefs, ideas, stories) need to be deleted to allow me to move forward?

4. What does an upgraded version of me look like?

CHAPTER 10.

TIME TO PRIORITISE.

I've been watching a series about time travel. It is all about how certain events impact the future and how even though the characters travel back in time, there are some things even they can't control. Yes, I know it is a fictional story, but I do take from it that we don't control how much time we have available on earth, but we hold how we experience our time here. I always tell my children that things will happen to us in life that we can't control. The only thing we do control is how we choose to react to whatever happens to us in life. This is a complicated concept for a 12- and 14-year-old to grasp. Especially in instances where they feel disappointed about something. Making choices gives us incredible control. A lesson I hope that they will get to understand when they are older.

With this in mind – how do you mindfully spend your time? And why don't we allow ourselves to live more intentionally? Intention without action stays but a dream. To dream is great, to be inspired drives us forward, but the trick is to keep the momentum going especially when the motivation starts to fizzle out.

It's time to stop thinking and start doing.

I don't know about you, but I've started many things that I have not finished. And every time that happens, it discourages me from even trying again in the future. I recently ran a leadership session for a group of people about self-discipline. While preparing for this session, and from these leaders' feedback, I was reminded of some truths that I would like to share.

Self-discipline is a DOing word. It is a daily choice. Motivation is excellent, but it is rarely sustainable if not supported by habits and rituals. Too much self-discipline may lead to burn-out, and too little self-discipline will lead to laziness. The sweet spot in the middle will lead to sustainability, longevity, and results. Understanding why you are doing something and adding meaning and emotion is essential. Add repetition to the mix, and the correct behaviour will follow, and it will become effortless.

Self-discipline is intentional. Success does not happen by accident. It takes hard work, commitment, failing, getting up, and pushing through the pain or discomfort. It is essential to work on your habit fitness. Remember that not everyone is at the same fitness level, so don't judge yourself or others.

My kids amaze me when it comes to self-discipline. I know they are not as disciplined in all areas of their lives, especially when it comes to home chores, but I can learn a lot from them regarding things that matter most to them, like athletics and hurdles specifically. Although they are only teenagers, they have clarity around their goals. They both want to be chosen for the South African athletics hurdle finals. They've attached meaning and emotion to their goal. They have a coach who has a training plan and breaks what needs to be done into smaller pieces. He understands the full picture and where he wants to take them. They need to show up and do the work, even if they do not feel like going to practice. When the boys do not feel motivated, we remind them about their why – why they are doing all the hard work now so that they can have a pay-off when they reach their goal. It is always their choice to practice or not and funnily enough, they usually choose to attend practice. They have support. They have our support. They support each other, but they also support their teammates, who suffer and sweat alongside them during practice. Even though they may compete against each other in races, they have each other's best interests at heart and have a real bond – it is beautiful to see.

I'll never forget the time when my eldest faced a series of setbacks in his athletic pursuits. Most people would've given up, but not him. His commitment and self-discipline persevered through a string of unfortunate events. He broke his foot during the first season after falling out of a tree, and then the COVID-19 pandemic wreaked havoc on the next two seasons. But even after contracting the virus, he kept practicing throughout the winter to hone his skills. Despite falling over a hurdle during one event and getting sick again just days before another, he still competed and eventually came in third place to earn provincial colours. His determination and can-do attitude are truly inspiring, and I feel so lucky to be his mom.

Goals in action.

If you genuinely want to achieve your goals, you must commit and put in the work. I've created this section to allow you to do your work, reflect on some questions, take stock of where you are, where you want to be and why it is important for you, and what it will take to get you there. I will guide you by breaking it down into bite-size pieces so that you can focus on the work to be done.

Time to create stepping-stone goals.

I've struggled with setting realistic goals for myself in the past. It seems I've often set my sights too high, leading to feelings of failure and disappointment. For example, I've always wanted to be a runner, but with my hip replacement, I know that running a marathon may not be a realistic goal for me. Still, I'm not giving up on the idea entirely and have started running again, albeit more cautiously this time. Unfortunately, my enthusiasm got the best of me, and I ended up overdoing it on my first run back, which set me back. I've learned that having a clear vision for your future is essential, but it's equally important to remember that the journey towards that vision is just as crucial.

Some people say that you need to spend about 10 000 hours becoming an expert in something. But 10 000 hours is a lot! My friend always says: "My soul is in a hurry." I do not have the patience to do this. Yet, if you think about it, a baby does not start running, but it first sits, then crawls, stands, walks and runs. And every time that it falls, it is encouraged to try again and try again.

We somehow lose this ability as adults. We also lose the cheerleaders who push us to try and try and try again. People who help us get up when we fall. The Japanese proverb rings so true: "Vision without action is a daydream. Action without vision is a nightmare."

Rather than big unreachable goals, I want to argue that we should have bite-size goals that become our stepping stones to achieve our ultimate vision.

You probably know about the 10-Percent Rule[23] if you are a runner. When you start to run, you need to condition your body not to injure yourself. A common injury is IT Band Syndrome,[24] where the iliotibial band, a long piece of connective tissue that runs from your outer hip to your knee, gets irritated and inflamed due to doing too much too fast.

The 10-Percent Rule states that you should only increase your weekly running distance by a maximum of 10 percent. This allows your body to build capacity for more. The same applies to goals. You need to prime yourself for success to avoid injuries along the way and give yourself the best chance. You can also call these better-than-nothing goals. (Better to do something and fail than do nothing at all.)

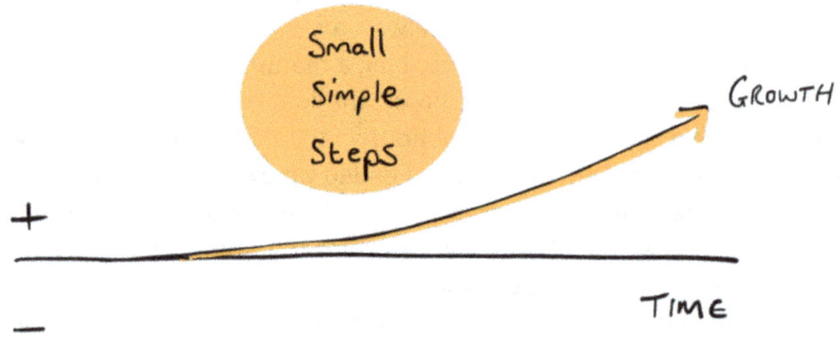

Small steps over time

[23] Burfoot, Amby. "The 10-Percent Rule." *Runner's World*, Runner's World, 3 Mar. 2022, https://www.runnersworld.com/training/a20781512/the-10-percent-rule/.

[24] Benjamin Wedro, MD. "It Band Syndrome Treatment, Symptoms, Recovery Time." *MedicineNet*, MedicineNet, 4 Mar. 2022, https://www.medicinenet.com/iliotibial_band_syndrome/article.htm.

Become an "itamae" of your own agile life.

Sushi chefs are called 'itamae'[25] in Japan. This is a prestigious job and becoming an itamae takes years and years of dedication, training, and hard work. To become an itamae, you need to start right at the bottom – from being a cleaner to a rice maker before finally gaining the apprenticeship called 'wakiita', meaning 'near the cutting board'. After many years they may receive the title of itamae if they are deemed good enough and receive their own set of sushi knives called 'hocho'.

The Japanese culture, rooted in honour and respect, is the basis for an itamae who needs to handle their ingredients, knives, and customers with precision, charm, and grace.

I use the analogy of an itamae to illustrate that it takes time and small steps to reach the end goal. To realise that many bite-size goals rather than one BIG goal will get you there.

I don't know about you, but I was not too fond of sushi the first time I had it. My brother took my then boyfriend and me to this fantastic well-known sushi restaurant in the Waterfront in Cape Town.

He probably spent a lot of money on us being students then, who didn't even appreciate the sushi, specifically the sashimi, raw fish, just sounded terrible at the time. The problem was my inability to look past the raw fish. I was caught up in my head and limited my experience to change and try something new.

Now, years later, I can eat sushi every single day. What changed? My willingness to try something new. My ability to appreciate new taste sensations. And, of course – my love for wasabi, soya, and ginger!

---

[25] Admin. "Why It Takes a Decade of Training to Be a Head Sushi Chef." *Kobe Jones*, 14 Mar. 2017, https://www.kobejones.com.au/why-it-takes-a-decade-of-training-to-be-a-head-sushi-chef/.

With this in mind, ask yourself the following questions.
1. How do you become the Itamae of your own life?
2. What steps do you need to take and what habits do you need to cultivate to continuously improve to achieve the ultimate title of Itamae in your life?

To help you determine where you should focus your attention or prioritise your bite-size goals, you need to have a look at your life in total.

The Japanese have a lunch box that they call a 'bento box'.[26] This lunch box is made of plastic or lacquered wood divided into different compartments or sections filled with various dishes.

Our life consists of different 'compartments,' like a bento box. It is like a symphony of food when all the tastes come together. But it is an art to perfect the balance and combinations. Sometimes it is hard to balance what is good for us with what we want most.

In life, we often prioritise the wrong things without even realising it. It is time to assess and refocus on which moments or areas of our lives matter most to us; to determine where we should focus more or less, and to assist us in choosing our goals.

* * *

Me time.

It is now time to reflect. We all know what is most important to us in life. If we then look at how much time we spend on or prioritise the things we say are important, there is sometimes a disconnect. The following exercise will help you identify and prioritise more mindfully.

---

[26] "Bento Boxes: Kids Web Japan." *Web Japan*, https://web-japan.org/kidsweb/virtual/bento/bento04.html.

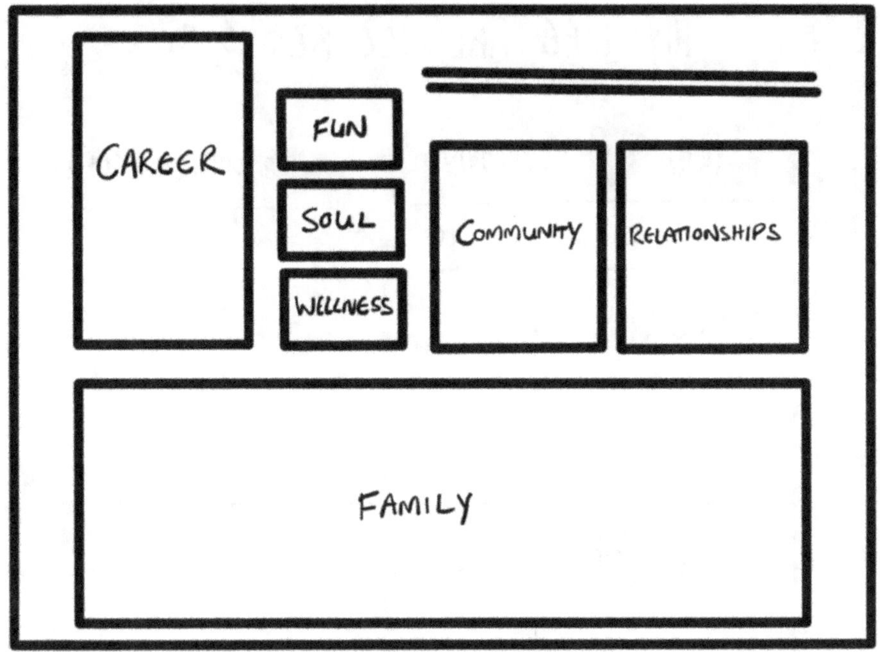

My Bento balance box.

Reflect on the following questions.

1. Do a bento balance life box assessment and answer the questions on the next page. Look at the following areas of your life and decide how much space it takes up in your bento box of life.

- Career (my job)
- Fun (anything that brings me joy or makes me smile)
- Community (actively involved in either my direct community where I live or a community where I share a similar interest like a hobby for instance)
- Spirituality (anything that fills your soul)
- Relationships (friends, colleagues or romantic)
- Wellness (this includes physical and mental health and overall well-being)
- Family (my direct family)

MY LIFE BALANCE BENTO BOX

AREA	RATING 1-10	ACTIONS TO GROW
CAREER		
FUN		
COMMUNITY		
SPIRITUALITY		
RELATIONSHIPS		
WELLNESS		
FAMILY		

2. Look at your life balance bento box. Is there any space or spaces in your bento box that you would like to grow or want to prioritise?

130

3. If yes, jot down a couple of practical things that you can do right now to grow it by 1 percent per day.

CHAPTER 11.

TIME FOR INTENTIONAL GOALS.

I've learned that intent and motivation alone are not enough. Reaching your goals takes self-discipline and continuous action. The best advice I can give you is to schedule time for your goals. Please put the actions that will bring you closer to your goals in your calendar and stick to it. I even set alarms for myself on my cellphone. And ask yourself the question – what is the cost of spending the time and the cost of not spending the time on your goals?

Be realistic and honest when setting goals so that you do not set yourself up for failure. If you struggle to get out of bed and walk around the block, start with a smaller goal that is viable. Your long-term goal may be to run the Comrades Marathon, but your first goal should be to walk for 1 km, then run 1 km, then 5 km, then 10 km, and only then do you reach for the stars. It is like building blocks. You don't build a wall in one go; you start by laying one brick correctly – one step at a time to reach great heights.

Failing at something does not mean the end. It is merely one step closer to building up stamina and skill to get to where you need to be.

Recipe to 'unchallenge' a goal.

I want to encourage you to spend some time on the following with me. Put away your cellphone or any distractions and focus on yourself and your vision for yourself for a moment. Journal on the following questions. Be open to whatever comes up for you. Take your time.

Think about a specific goal you have that you've been struggling with, whether at work or in life in general.

The goal.

1. Why is this goal important to me?

2. How will I feel when I achieve my goal?

3. What is preventing me from reaching the goal?

Let's time travel together.

We are going to do a visualisation exercise for a moment. When we visualise, we allow ourselves to really focus on what is important. We tap into all our senses and may unlock what we already know is true for us. It allows a space to focus on what is most important to us.

Suspend all judgment and, for a moment, take a nice deep breath in and out and just do a quick body scan. Do you have any tension in your face, your shoulders, your back? Take another deep breath in and with the breath out, let go of any stress and tension. (Close your eyes while you do this body scan to really tap into how you feel in this moment.)

Now, imagine for a moment, a time travel machine. See it from the outside. What does it look like? Climb into the machine. What do you see?

Press the green button that is labelled FUTURE. The machine comes to life. There are sounds and lights and you start to travel into the future. You land on a planet. What do you see on this planet? What are the colours, the sounds, the smells?

Imagine that you meet your future self who has already accomplished the goal you set. You sit down with your future self.

1. Where are you meeting your future self?
2. What do the surroundings look like?
3. How do you feel meeting your future self?
4. What is your future you wearing?
5. Is there anyone else with you or are you alone?
6. What else do you see around you?
7. What do you hear, smell, feel?
8. Ask your future you how you overcame obstacles to reach the goal.
9. Ask your future you what practical steps you took to reach the goal.
10. Ask your future you to give you any gifts that may help you on your journey.

Now say thank you to your future self and take the gifts your future self gave you. Get into the time machine and press the yellow button labelled PRESENT and travel back to the present time.

With this newfound knowledge, write down the wisdom you received from your future self and anything that you've discovered during your time travel in your journal.

* * *

Me Time.

It is now time to reflect. We all have goals and habits that either serve our goals or distract us from them. Get clarity around your goals and find habits that will get you closer to them. Remember that intention will stay only 'intention' if you don't choose to design and act on it. Dream it. Plan it. Create routines to support it and take action!

Use the template on the next page to make notes and add additional notes in your journal should you need more thinking and writing space.

Reflect on the following.

1. **What is the goal:** What is the change I seek? Be very specific.

2. **Prioritise:** What do I want to focus on first? Sort the priorities into things that give me the most energy.

3. **Clarity:** Why do I need to achieve this? What will the outcome be?

4. **Structure:** Work smarter not harder – put a plan in place that is doable and realistic

5. **Cost:** what will I deny myself if I don't do this?

6. **Accountability:** What habits will support my goal and help me to keep my momentum going and how will I keep myself accountable?

7. **Celebrate:** How will I celebrate my success?

Now that you understand your why, it is time to break your goal down into smaller pieces, get support if needed, and always remember why you want to do this. I've found that if you do not schedule time for your goal, it will stay on this page. Make one commitment to yourself this week to get you closer to your goal. Put that commitment in your calendar or set a reminder on your phone.

MY COMMITMENT TO ME

COMMITMENT	ACTION	DATE

WHY IS IT IMPORTANT

COST OF NOT FOLLOWING THROUGH

MY GOAL

MY COMMITMENTS

GOAL PLANNING

MY WORRIES AND CONCERNS
MY GOAL
DATE
STEP 4
STEP 3
STEP 2
STEP 1

CHAPTER 12.

TIME TO HATCH SOME HABITS.

There are a lot of different views in terms of breaking old habits or creating new patterns. Some say it takes 28 days to form a new habit, some 40 days. Some believe it can take a second or a lifetime. Whatever you believe, all habits consist of three parts. It is called a habit loop that consists of a cue, a routine, and a reward.

The best chance you have to rewire your brain, which is amazingly possible up to the day you die, is to understand the cue, change the routine or behaviour, and keep the reward. Let me explain this through an example that is easy to relate to.

The cue for me was some me-time before the day started. I used to love to lie in bed in the mornings scrolling through Facebook to see what I had missed. To see whose birthday was coming up or get ideas on what activities to do with the kids or new places to discover. The problem with this habit is that it made my brain reactive and took away my creativity. It was also too time-consuming and made the pace of the rest of the morning intense. So, I changed the routine and decided not to look at my phone for the first 30 minutes after getting up. I also started to wake up 30 minutes earlier to either do some exercise or mindfulness or a gratitude exercise to get me ready for the day. The reward is still my me-time, but I now feel much more creative and energized in the mornings.

To achieve your goal, you will need to get fit (mind and body), so think about the habits that will support your dream. Stop finding excuses not to do something and focus on why you should do it. Shift your focus to what you will gain rather than what you may need to give up or let go of.

The most successful people in the world have many things that they do that they are more than happy to share. You may know some of these things, but it is always great to be reminded and recommit to doing things for yourself.

Think about your current habits – the positive and less positive habits. What are your habit cues (the triggers), the routines (behaviours) and rewards? Can you think of any habit where you can tweak the behaviours that do not serve you? What impact will this have on you?

It has been suggested that Aristotle said: "We are what we repeatedly do. Excellence, then, is not an act, but a habit."[27]

Recipe: More Me – how to expand you.

Think about your morning routine, or as I like to call it – more-me routine. Do you leave it up to chance, or do you plan it?

Is the routine healthy or unhealthy? Here are a couple of ideas I gathered from the most successful people around the world when it comes to mornings:

- Make your bed so that you start the day with a win.
- Brush your teeth with the opposite hand to stimulate a different part of your brain.
- Drink a glass of water with some lemon juice to activate your body.
- Take a shower (this is where creative ideas happen – when your brain is in a theta state).
- End your shower with a cold shower to reset your nervous system. (I struggle with this one!)
- Journal or reflect on your intentions for the day. What are you grateful for, and what are three things you want to accomplish, whether big or small, for the day?
- Eat brain foods, such as avocados, blueberries, greens, eggs and nuts.
- Read (even for only 10–20 minutes).

---

[27] Sylvester, Brad. "Fact Check: Did Aristotle Say, 'We Are What We Repeatedly Do'?" *Check Your Fact*, Check Your Fact, 26 June 2019, https://checkyourfact.com/2019/06/26/fact-check-aristotle-excellence-habit-repeatedly-do/.

- Meditate (or practice mindfulness when you do your everyday tasks like making sandwiches for the kids or washing the dishes. The key is to be present in the moment.).
- Exercise even if just for 10–15 minutes in the morning.
- No phones in the first 30 minutes in the morning – you are training your brain for distraction and being reactive if you check your phone first thing in the morning. Instead, use this time to build your brain.

How to prioritise you.

1. Do your work first. Prioritise yourself, your goals, rituals, and habits.
2. Block time in your calendar for you, or others will.
3. If possible, do this in the morning when you are fresh and energised. (You may think that you are not a morning person, but if you get enough sleep, this may shift for you.)
4. Set intentions for the day – what will you do, what will you not do and how will you be today?
5. Get an accountability partner. You do not have to go at this alone. Get support from people you trust and respect who will hold you accountable.
6. It does not have to be your partner or best friend. Let them remind you why you are doing this in the first place, especially when it becomes challenging.
7. Get a support buddy. The difference between an accountability partner and a support buddy is that your support buddy is only there for you. They do not have to remind you of anything or keep you accountable. They are just there as your cheerleader – a shoulder to cry on when things do not go your way or to celebrate your small and big successes.
8. Rewards and celebrations. Celebrate publicly (i.e., invite a friend out for a drink to celebrate a milestone with you). Let someone share in the win. Remember why you are doing this! Reward yourself for every milestone reached – even the small ones.

Better than nothing habits.

Have you ever had the best intentions to change an unhealthy habit into a healthy habit and then fell short in the implementation phase? It may have started off great and then fizzled out?

We all do this, so please do not judge yourself. The invitation is to do one thing that will have a positive impact on you. Think small. One small thing that you can change. Do it and celebrate the win. It could be that you walk your dog around the block every day before you binge-watch a series on TV. Or, maybe instead of snacking on a whole slab of chocolate you buy better quality dark chocolate and have three blocks instead. Better than nothing habits help you to maintain consistency. And by consistently doing something, it will become an effortless habit that may lead to bigger changes over time. For example, once I start to walk the dog every day, I will get fitter, feel better and may be open to walk further than just the three blocks for instance.

What is one small thing you can do that is a better than nothing action that can inform your habits in the future?

Think about your current routine and habits.

1. How are your habits supporting you to reach your goals?

2. Which habits do you need to amend or change?

3. Which new habits do you need to focus on more?

4. What is the impact of your habits on you?

5. Is there anything you would like to do differently?

Having habits in place that support you reaching your goals is so important. If you truly want something, go after it, and put the systems in place to help you get there. Changing your reality is your responsibility – own it!

***

Me Time.

Let's hatch our habits!

Use the template on the next page to make notes and add additional notes in your own journal should you need more thinking and writing space.

Make sure that whatever commitments you make to yourself are reachable and measurable. Also, remember to schedule these commitments in your calendar to allow for them to become your new way of being and doing.

Reflect on the following.

1. What did I discover about myself and my current habits?

2. What habits need to be expired?

3. What commitment will I make for the next 10 days to form new more-me habits?

4. What habits need to be in place to support my goal and help me to keep my momentum going?

5. What commitments am I making to myself?

HABIT	BENEFIT	REWARD

CHAPTER 13.

TIME TO GROW AND LET GO – MY IMPACT.

I believe that there are two kinds of people: People who see their problems as unfixable, and people who view problems as possibilities and opportunities.

A person with a closed state of mind usually believes that their past determines their future and believes they have no power to change anything. They limit their growth and learning by looking at situations as either black or white. "I am not good at this, so I won't even try." Or they may give up easily when they get frustrated. They stop when something is complex and stick to what they know. Their comfort zone gives them a sense of security.

A person with an open mindset is the opposite. They know that failure is a way to learn and grow and that challenges push them to be better despite it being hard and uncomfortable. An open state of mind means that abilities are directly linked to attitude and effort. They welcome feedback as they know they can learn and be better. They understand that there is always a lesson to learn or gold to be found when things go wrong.

The gold is the gifts, lessons and experiences that make us better. It is that silver lining around a cloud or the rainbow during a storm. It is the ability to focus on the good in bad situations. To look past the negative and to find the lesson and wisdom it offers.

This always makes me think of the cartoon image of the man sitting on a train that passes a massive wall on one side and a beautiful view on the other. This guy sits looking only at the wall and misses the beauty and splendour of nature altogether.

If he had only tilted his head to the left, his whole journey could have been more exciting and filled with joy and beauty. I believe the same applies in life – where you focus and what you choose to see will determine the reality and quality of your life.

Brazilian artist Genildo Ronchi, August 2013 – "As vezes só depende de nós" which translates to: "Sometimes it just depends on us."[28]

Small tweaks can pivot the course of your life.

Our life is the sum total of the choices we make. We don't always need to take major action, but rather make minor tweaks or adjustments, test, re-test, and do the work. To illustrate this, I want to tell you a quick story:

When my younger son started to run hurdles, he picked it up without effort and ran beautifully. Then he practised the starting position and all was well. But as he progressed in the races, he was forced to start using starting blocks at national competitions and this became a hurdle in its own right.

---

[28] Schroeder, Audra. "What Is the 'Two Guys on a Bus' Meme?" *The Daily Dot*, 23 Nov. 2021, https://www.dailydot.com/unclick/two-guys-on-a-bus-meme/.

Hurdles are quite a technical sport, so when he had to run with starting blocks for the first time, his steps were out of rhythm to the first hurdle, which meant he could not run as usual. It was frustrating and we could not figure it out. I decided to problem solve this with the help of his elder brother, Eben.

We set off to the track one Sunday to help Louis. We tried everything. We counted the steps. We changed the starting block settings. We got frustrated and irritated. And then, Eben and I stepped away from Louis for a while to leave him to try things by himself. And when I watched him from afar, I realised something. I asked Eben which leg he used to go over the first hurdle and as he is left-handed, he would use his right leg to go over the first hurdle. Louis is right-handed. When I looked at him again with this newfound information, I saw that he was also going over with his right leg first. It then dawned on us that, without the starting blocks, he usually used his left leg over the first hurdle. With the introduction of the starting blocks, this changed. So, we adjusted his starting blocks and where his left foot used to be at the back of the blocks, we switched it around making it possible for him to get over the hurdle with his left leg first. A minor adjustment that made all the difference. We never had to worry about starting blocks and the first hurdle ever again!

Sometimes the smallest changes have the biggest impact. Most athletes know this – the golfers who make a millimetre change on their club grip to hit the perfect put; the cyclists who set up their bicycles to the exact measurements of their body, and the impact on their performance if they get that wrong. There are many examples of this.

Think about a small change you can make in your life that will have a huge impact down the line.

Being imperfectly perfect.

Remember the Japanese tradition where they use a particular art form to mend broken pottery with a specific glue covered in gold dust? It is called 'Kintsugi', which means golden joinery. They believe that rather than disguising the brokenness of an object, they should mend it in a way that shows its history. It also symbolises the idea that you can always begin again even if you failed in the past. It is a symbol of growth, learning from past mistakes and hope. Isn't that fantastic? Celebrating the brokenness and making it not just acceptable, but beautiful.

I wish that we could do this with humans as well. I am saddened by our school system that instils fear and shame in our kids and later adults if mistakes are made or people's actions are imperfect. We are imperfect. We make mistakes. We are human. But rather than hiding these mistakes away, we should learn from them, mend them and be proud of the learning. We are not broken. We are human. We are a Kintsugi bowl in the making.

The balancing act in life.

I've been fortunate to speak to many different people from all over the world and the common theme I see everywhere is the issue with balance. More specifically, Work-Life-Balance. We all struggle with it, but if we don't make an effort to get the balance back and maintain it, this will stay our reality.

I once had someone in a workshop tell me that they believe people need to leave their problems and issues at home when they come to work. She was not a mean or bad person, but she was so end-goal-focused that the rest did not matter.

The problem with the end goal only focus is that we get tunnel vision and miss the bigger picture. I was shocked and saddened that we've created this thinking norm in the business world.

In many cases, work is a place where you are expected to walk through the door to work, like a robot, and are stripped of all emotions when you enter and that you can pick up on your way out of the door at 5 pm. In a way, I understood her frustration, and I agree that we do need to take more ownership of our emotions and our responsibilities. But to ignore feelings is like putting them in a pressure cooker without that little valve that allows the steam out. At some stage, those feelings will blow. If we purge them more often, the blow may be softened or will not take place at all. The only way to purge is to acknowledge our feelings, talk more about them, and have more empathy for ourselves and others.

The thing with emotions is that they make us human. And they do drive behaviour. If a company expects people to come to work without feeling, they are kidding themselves.

People are good at suppressing emotions, but emotions do not go away. Listening to and acknowledging feelings without fixing them may seem counterproductive but is good enough. To normalise emotions is a skill I wish we could teach kids and adults alike.

I genuinely believe that you CANNOT leave your heart at home when you go to work.

This reminds me of a story of a man who walked home from work daily. In front of his home was a beautiful big oak tree. Every day he would walk to his home, stop at the big oak tree, and stand there for five minutes before going inside his house.

One day a neighbour, who was watering his garden, and who saw this happening day after day, stopped him and asked him why he did it. He replied that he took everything that happened that day at work that brought him down and hung it onto the tree, enabling him to be fully present for his kids at home without any baggage from work. I love this. It is taking care of ourselves first to enable us to take better care of others. Remember when you last flew on an airplane, and they told you that, in a case of emergency, to place your mask on yourself before you help younger kids? You have to help yourself before you can help others. That way there is more of you to give.

Recipe for a more fulfilling life.

So why do I tell you all of this? If we want to grow, we need to be super aware of the following.

1. Firstly, we need to be open to possibilities and to see opportunities when they cross our paths. If you are not looking for it, you may well miss what is right in front of you. That is why it is super important to have a growth mindset. You become what you focus on.
2. We need to learn from our mistakes and try something even if it scares us. Courage means that we push through even if something scares us. It means that we rather try and fail than fail to try.
3. We need to have emotional intelligence, acknowledge our emotions, and empathise with others. This is what makes us human, and rather than ignoring emotions, we should be mindful and curious about what sits behind our emotions or the emotions of others. When we acknowledge and accept emotions, we are one step closer to knowing ourselves and others better. To be vulnerable will give others the courage to also show up, fully human.
4. We need to be clear about our goals and then we need to take action and make the efforts sustainable through discipline and the choices we make. It is important to have goals, but more importantly is to have sustainable and continuous structures or habits in place to drive you forward. To keep the momentum going even on the days when the motivation or inspiration is low.

It is time to uncover or rediscover your life purpose. The meaning of you. The balancing act of both what you do in life and how you show up whilst doing what you do.

* * *

Me Time.

It is now time to reflect. Why do you get out of bed every morning? What gives you energy and what is your purpose in life? By completing the following exercise, you may get answers about your reason for being.

Use the template on the next page to make notes and add additional notes in your journal should you need more thinking and writing space.

Reflect on the following – my impact statement.

Let's uncover YOU. Remember that this is a journey and the ideal. You may never get there 100 percent, but even if you aim for the moon, you may reach the stars!

Step 1.
How I show up (being).
1. What makes me want to jump out of bed in the morning that gives me joy? (my true passion)

2. What is important enough for me to take a stand for in life? (making the world better and contributing beyond myself)

What I do (doing).

3. What is my superpower or skill? (This can be any talent or skill I have even if it falls outside of my day job.)

4. What is the job I do daily? (What am I getting paid for?)

My legacy (impact).
5. What do I want others to say about me when I am gone? (How do I want to make them feel?)

Step 2.
Underline or circle the words in each of your answers above that stand out for you.

Step 3.
Combine the words you identified as most important and write down a sentence or word that describes the essence of you. How do you want to show up in all areas of your life?

Complete your life purpose statement:

I want to (doing) ...

By showing up with (my being) ...

So that (impact) ...

Now that you have clarity about your true self, let's give it some energy.

6. Write down three things that you give yourself license to do/be/have. Your permit to a balanced life.

BEING

DOING

IMPACT

MY PURPOSE

PERMISSION TO:

DO _______________________

BE _______________________

HAVE _______________________

III.

DOING THE WORK TO MAKE MY DREAMS COME TRUE.

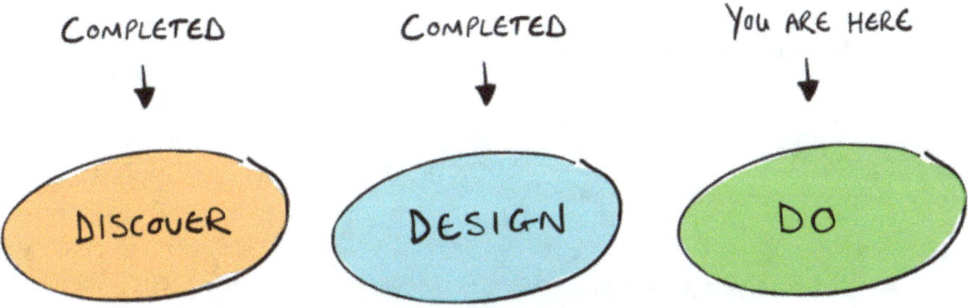

In this section we will put your design plan into action to make your dreams become a reality.

Before we dive in, let's answer the following questions. Circle your answer.

1. I procrastinate on my goals.

Agree   Sometimes   Disagree

2. I tend to lose focus and momentum after focusing on a goal for a while.

Agree   Sometimes   Disagree

3. I struggle to ask for help.

Agree   Sometimes   Disagree

4. I set healthy boundaries.

Agree   Sometimes   Disagree

5. I understand the importance of practicing gratitude.

Agree   Sometimes   Disagree

CHAPTER 14.

TIME FOR ACTION.

Congratulations! You've been working hard on your life. Uncovering and rediscovering the real you. Keep going. You've got this.

You may have had different feelings as we've gone on this journey, but I want to remind you again that nothing is wrong with you. You are not broken or need fixing. You are a whole, resourceful, exceptional and creative human being.

Have you ever seen someone tune a piano? They do it with such passion. The person doing it really listens with an exercised and tuned-in ear making minor adjustments with love. This is your journey to tune your life. Once you understand who you are at the core, you can control your external world so much better.

You may say to me that time is the main reason for procrastination. "I feel overwhelmed." "There are not enough hours in the day." Or "I am too thinly spread." I hear you! It is all true. I've also felt this way and still do some days.

In life, you have many different roles to fulfil and thus need to juggle many things. Work, home, family, friends, kids, animals, responsibilities – you name it. You are juggling all these many different things. A coach once asked me if any of these many things I was juggling had to drop, which would be glass balls that would break on impact, and which would bounce back even if I dropped them? This question put into perspective what to prioritise in my life. I want you to think of the same question. Once you've identified your glass balls, it is up to you to take decisive action to prevent your glass balls from shattering.

Procrastination busters.

Once-off motivation without repetitive action is what happens to most of us. We get swept up and ready to do something and may even start with a project, an idea, an exercise programme, or whatever is most pressing at that moment, but in the end, it fizzles out and we default to the old way. The ways that do not serve us. Our default state. That place of comfort and path of least resistance. This is the place where your life is on autopilot and where you have no control. It may seem easier here with much less effort, but is this the type of life you dreamed of?

I was thinking about this when I spoke to my coach in Russia. I am South African and very Afrikaans, but I met a fantastic coach from Russia in a workshop we both attended (this was about a year before Russia invaded Ukraine). We made a deal. She would practice her coaching skills and English on me, and I could talk through the things in life where I felt stuck.

In one of our sessions, we spoke about how I've been sitting on work needing to be done. I was procrastinating and finding excuses not to do it, because of my insecurities.

The task at hand was to create and then video record content for an online course on the skill of handling conflict with confidence. I love researching and creating content that can help people, but to put this into context, I am no actor! I feel uncomfortable in front of a camera, and I cringe every time I see and hear myself on recordings – it does not come naturally, and I have a deep admiration for people and actors who do this for a living. This was during the COVID-19 period, so I was flying solo. I had to create the content, record it, and edit it in my home and makeshift studio setup, so it was a brand-new experience for me.

My coach and I unpacked the real reasons for my procrastination. I discovered that what was keeping me back was not the makeshift setup or limited video knowledge, but mainly self-doubt and something called imposter syndrome (where you do not feel worthy or skilled enough wondering if you will be caught out and seen as an imposter).

During our coaching sessions we shifted the focus on why I wanted and needed to complete the task. She asked questions about the cost of not finishing the task in both time and money. She reminded me of the time lost and the lives that could have been touched through this content if I had just gotten over my insecurities and finished the recordings.

This motivated me to shift my focus to the end result and impact of the task, rather than on the barriers that kept me from completing it. She kept reminding me about my own values of kindness and care, and once we linked these values to the output of the task, it was easy.

BUT the motivation in and of itself is not enough. There is also something called continuous action. Moving forward and not getting stuck again. So, in the last part of the session, I had to commit to three steps to reach my goal. I had to set an intention in terms of how I wanted to feel and how I wanted other people to feel when they saw my final product and I had to give a specific date to complete the task. I then needed to send confirmation of completion to my coach and my boss.

With motivation comes accountability. And this, in turn, keeps the focus and the continuous action. I finished the recordings on the same day. It took a whole day to complete, but I felt proud, connected, and focused. Where it once seemed impossible and daunting, it now felt natural and easy – a real turnaround for me.

Put the energy back into action.

I've also learned that energy plays a HUGE role in the action. When you feel tired, stressed, overwhelmed, or overworked and your body has low energy, you do not feel like doing anything.

The first step is to get energy back into your body, because energy creates energy. One way to create energy is through healthy living. I'm not saying you need to start running a marathon or becoming a vegetarian, but not living by default means you need to choose to focus on eating, sleeping, and movement.

I joined a challenge where I stopped eating sugar, coffee, processed food and alcohol for ten days. I also drank green veggie juice and beetroot juice that I made for myself and a lot of fresh non-processed food and minimal carbohydrates for ten days. You may be reading this thinking – no way. I will never do this. I was there, so I know how you feel. I also thought it was crazy, but I opened myself up to the possibility of doing it. I had an open mindset about it.

I drank a lot of water, starting with a glass of water and lemon first thing in the morning. Once the ten days were up, I craved fresh food and juices and felt much more alive, healthy, and energized. The cells in my body were ecstatic about the healthy food and could excel and move around more freely. I was also surprised that I did not crave sugar, as I used to be a real chocoholic. The trick is that when you try and quit something, there is a sense of loss and giving something up. Focusing on what you gain and not the pain of giving anything up, is a game changer. After three weeks, I had my first cup of coffee and felt terrible afterwards. My head was spinning; my heart was racing; it was awful. So, the choice is easy; coffee does not serve me at the moment. This may change in the future. I'm not saying I will never drink coffee again, but I am happy with tea or water for now.

I started to move more. With lockdown during the COVID-19 Pandemic, we all began to sit in front of screens most of the time. We did not walk to our cars in the parking lot or from our desks to meeting rooms. We moved so much less than we used to move before COVID-19, a staggering fact and a good motivator for me.

I learned about something called 'Egoscue'. It is a form of stretching and on-the-spot exercises that help with posture and aligning and balancing your major joints and body. I also did a bit of 'Qigong', a gentle movement and mindfulness exercise. And I started to run again. Not very far or fast, but just getting my heart rate up a bit.

Sleep into action.

The next focus was sleep. We all know that sleeping is essential. It affects our immune system, helps prevent weight gain, strengthens your heart and improves memory.

It gives our body a chance to regenerate cells and muscles to heal after major exercise and many other positives.

Did you know that when you sleep for only four hours a night studies show that your killer cells – your immune system – drops by a staggering 70 percent?[29]

Have you ever gone to sleep with a problem or issue and then woken up with a solution the next day? The reason for this is that our brains never stop working. When deep asleep, our brain processes our new memories into long-term storage.

I don't know about you, but I've had times when I did not sleep enough and then felt groggy, numb, and unfocused the next day. This is explained by the following piece that surprised me most in reading up on sleep. It seems that when we sleep, our brains get a chance to make new connections and processing and physically get cleaned. Researchers think cerebrospinal

---

[29] "How to Sleep Better." *MasterClass*, MasterClass, 18 Mar. 2022, https://www.masterclass.com/classes/matthew-walker-teaches-the-science-of-better-sleep/chapters/how-to-sleep-better?utm_source%3DEmail.

fluid (CSF) may flush toxic waste out, 'cleaning' the brain.[30] This clearance of toxins is hugely improved by sleep. It is almost like our brains are taking a shower while we sleep!

An intention recipe.

The next part of my new habit-forming for energy and sustainability was a more precise and focused morning or more-me routine.

I started mindfulness habits where I focus on setting my intentions for the day.

Write down three things: What I want to do, to be and to feel today. Some days I do a guided meditation practice – there are many excellent resources online or meditation apps, or I am mindful and am present with small mundane things like making and drinking green juice or washing dishes. Feel the vegetables as you cut them, smell them, taste them – hear the birds singing in the trees outside. Take small sips. Be present.

I want to invite you to try it for 14 days. Just 14 days and see the effect on your life. This is the first step in designing your life. Focus on the essential things and you will not be swept away by life happening.

Make looking after yourself a priority. Choose your lifestyle, as this will directly impact your quality of life. It is as easy or complex as you make it for yourself in your mind.

You are usually your biggest obstacle. The invitation is to get out of your own way by shifting your focus. Kick-start your energy and focus on the impact of the choices you make and the actions you take.

* * *

---

[30] Makin, Simon. "Deep Sleep Gives Your Brain a Deep Clean." *Scientific American*, Scientific American, 1 Nov. 2019, https://www.scientificamerican.com/article/deep-sleep-gives-your-brain-a-deep-clean1/.

Me Time.

It is now time to reflect.

1. What is keeping you from the things you want most in life?
2. What will your life be like and feel like if you could push through the obstacles?
3. And what are some actions you can take to own your future by dreaming, planning and being brave?

Let's uncover this together.

Use the template on the next page to make notes and add additional notes in your journal should you need more thinking and writing space.

Reflect on the following.

Think about a situation where you are stuck right now, at work or in your personal life. You know you should do something but always put it off, avoid it or ignore it.

Think about something you either wish you could do or have to do, but that you can't get a grip on – always finding excuses not to do.

Now, ask yourself these questions.

1. What is the cost of doing this? Maybe you need to spend more time on this and give up some of your leisure time; you may have to face your fears or even show some vulnerability in the process.

2. What is the cost of NOT doing this? Maybe if you don't do this, you
   may have regrets, feel like a failure, or feel like an imposter.

3. What are some of the choices and habits that will help you
   overcome the barriers and be your procrastination busters in life?

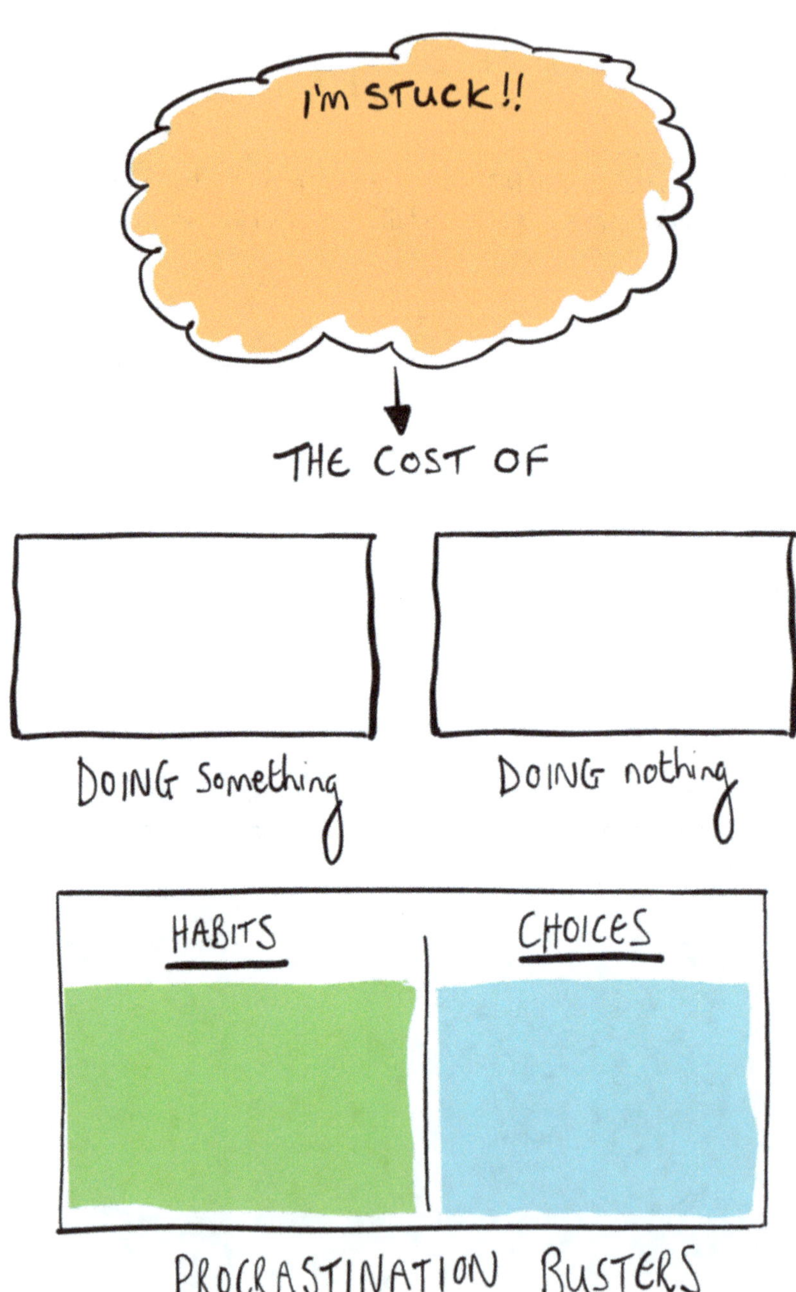

I'M STUCK!!
THE COST OF
DOING something
DOING nothing
HABITS
CHOICES
PROCRASTINATION BUSTERS

CHAPTER 15.

TIME FOR SUPPORT.

My husband is a huge F1 Grand Prix fan. I used to lie on the couch and watch it with him in our early years of marriage before we had kids, and it was usually the best naps I ever had! I liked it, but the sound of the cars going around for such a long time was the best sleeping pill for me. I understand that it takes skill, strategy and, most of all, teamwork in the pit stops. When a team of people pull together, everyone focuses on their part to make the whole work.

In a recent race, there was a horrific crash. The racer lost control and hit a wall at 220 kmph at 53 g's (G-force). To put this in perspective – when you go around a corner at a very high speed in a car, you can probably get to about 3 g's. Fighter pilots can pull around 7–9 g's when they turn left or right and most people who are not used to this will pass out because of the blood rushing from their heads. This guy pulled 53 g's! That is insane!

His car broke in half on impact and the vehicle was instantly engulfed in flames. The French race car driver, Romain Grosjean, was still strapped in and a new safety feature in cars called the 'halo' saved his life.

The halo is a driver crash-protection system consisting of a curved titanium bar to protect the driver's head. This titanium cage can withstand many tons of weight to protect the drivers. The drivers also have a plastic film strip on their visors pulled off during pit stops to ensure they can see clearly. There are many layers of these strips on the visors. After the crash, the driver, Romain, looked around and saw an orange glow and was unsure what it was. He then realised it was flames and started trying to get out of the halo cage but could not. He tried and tried, but the visor strips on his helmet started to melt, because of the extreme heat, so he could not see what he was doing. He tried and tried and went from fighting to realising this was it. He stared death in the face.

He then thought about his kids and wife and as a final attempt tried and succeeded in getting his shoulder through the gap, but his foot was still stuck. So, he had to slide back down again and pull with all his might to release his foot. His shoe stayed behind, but he was free and this time, he made his way out. In an interview after the incident, he said that he felt the hands of someone pulling him out and leading him away. At that moment, he knew he was not alone and would be okay. He walked away from a crash that should have killed him, with only minor burns on his hands and feet. I listened to the interview on the radio and saw it again on YouTube and this story touched me. This all happened in 28 seconds.

This incident reminded me that we all have a crew who will pull us from our life crashes from time to time. Even though we need to do some of the work, helping hands are willing to pull us out. We all need safety cars, ambulances and fire trucks standing by and ready for action.

Who is your pit crew? Who are your biggest fans? Who are the people that will run to a car in flames with fire extinguishers and pull you out? The best way to get new crew members in your life is to become someone else's crew member. Support others. Be there.

How to become part of a support crew.

The main struggle for most people I interact with seems to be communication. My kids learn to write, read and do the occasional presentations or orals at school, but the impact of communication and listening to understand and not react is not a skill taught to our kids. We teach kids to compete with each other or get the best grades in school. We teach them to listen to react when they put up their hand first with the correct answer.

I was in a workshop once where we did an exercise in pairs, where one person had to speak about something they were passionate about and the other had to listen only. You could not ask questions or interrupt and once the other person stopped talking, the listener could only ask: "Is there anything more?"

This is a simple exercise, but so powerful as it makes you realise that it is challenging not to start thinking about how you want to react and add your story to their story. Remember the part where Colleen Lightbody spoke about how our brain focuses on being self-centered and connecting our stories with others? So yes, you don't have massive control over this automated brain response. But with practice, I have found that you can train your brain to move the focus away from your self-centeredness and give others the space to speak and think. If I know someone is listening to me without judgment, interruption, and creating a space for me, I can think deeper.[31] Let me give you an example. Have you ever been in a conversation with a group where someone, usually an extrovert, has the most airtime and no one else gets a chance to speak? Or someone who speaks and is interrupted regularly by others and does not finish their story (or even start)?

The thing is that people are so keen to add their story to your story that you sometimes have to fight to get airtime. You cannot pause, even for a moment, to think even deeper about the subject you are speaking about. Our conversations are almost like a competition rather than a space for us to reflect, pause, and think more profound thoughts.

Listening in and of itself is a gift. My colleague always teases me and says that the Mossad (the Israeli national intelligence agency known for their interrogation skills) trained me because people tell me many things that are either funny, exotic or personal about themselves. Even random people I have only just met. I do not have Mossad training, but I found that most people are hungry to be heard. It is a rare thing. And when people get the chance, they grab it and tell me random stuff, because they have time to think and reflect. I love creating these thinking spaces for people. But I also struggle with this sometimes. It takes effort and absolute focus.

Recipe for listening to understand.
1. Start to listen to others from a place where you are curious to understand what is going on for them. What they see, feel, or experience.
2. Ask questions to clarify things that you are uncertain of.
3. Test assumptions you may have.
4. Create thinking spaces for those around you.

---

[31] KLINE, NANCY. *Time to Think: Listening to Ignite the Human Mind.* CASSELL, 2021.

Our internal stories create our reality.

Once you have mastered the skill of listening, it is time to start to communicate with others about the things that matter most to you. What you need, want, but may not get, and your internal stories. I believe that all people have superpowers in different shapes and forms, but the one superpower no one has is knowing what is going on in your head and heart, without you telling them. You can't expect them to know. If you want to build supportive relationships, you must ask for what you need. This is not about laying down demands but rather sharing with others what your heart needs. Just take note that if you have certain expectations from others, you need to have clarity by discussing or unpacking expectations - theirs and yours, to enable you to reach a clear agreement.

Another important thing to remember is that we tend to make other people's stories our own. Let me give you an example to illustrate. Let's say a colleague at work with whom you have a good relationship walks past without greeting you. Your brain instantly makes up stories. Remember the part where our brains become the best fictional writers ever from the chapter on storytelling? You may assume that you did something wrong or that they are mad at you about something you said or did. You may even come up with reasons why they are ignoring you. You make this your story. You make it about you. But most of the time, that is so far from the truth. They may simply be deep in thought or stressed about a presentation at work. It is their story. It is not your story. It is, however, important to check in with them if you value this relationship. It may sound something like this: "Hi Jack – I waved at you this morning in the corridor, and you just walked past me without acknowledging me. I value our relationship and instantly thought I may have done or said something to upset you. I just want to check in and find out if you are okay? And if we are okay?"

By checking our stories out, we can share our realities with each other, and this will lead to strong and supportive relationships.

Let's talk about boundaries for a moment.

I have always been a bit of a people pleaser. The burden is that I sometimes did things for others to please them, not disappoint them, hurt them or lose their friendship an ongoing struggle that I am working through. I never learned to set boundaries or say no, which is a skill, by the way. Not being able to say no is exhausting and most of the time, it leads to resentment and anger for not standing up for myself or, even worse, becoming someone I don't always like. Since I started this journey, I've learned that it is okay to say no respectfully and I even have a T-shirt that says: "NO is a full sentence."

Someone once told me that we never explain when we say yes, but we feel the need to clarify in detail when we say no. You do not have to explain. You can say no with a lot of love and respect. No is a full sentence and the more you do it, the easier it becomes.

The thing that I never realised was that if we set healthy boundaries, we are actually respectful to ourselves and others. By setting boundaries, we are crystal clear about what is okay and what is not okay for us. To articulate that to the people around us is really a gift. And if I say no from this new perspective, it is actually not so hard. Set some intentions for yourself in terms of your boundary-setting practice. This may help you get clarity around the things that are a definite NO or a definite YES as well as those grey areas in between.

My boundaries audit.

1. What did you say yes to that you regretted?

2. Why do you think you said yes?

3. What were you afraid of if you said "No"

4. What could a KIND "no" have looked like?

What are my boundaries?

Your relationship with disappointment.

As I am a recovering people pleaser this has been one of the hardest lessons for me to learn. This is a double-edged sword. On the one hand I do not ever want to disappoint anyone and on the other hand, I expect that people should not disappoint me. This is a huge expectation to have for myself and others and I am continuously setting myself and others up to fail, by having these unreasonable expectations.

The word 'disappointment' is such a loaded word. I had to learn to change my language around disappointment. I shifted it to – the outcome was not what I expected.

How would this perspective shift situations for you – how would you react and behave and feel?

Ultimately, it is not about what other people think about you, but more about what you think and feel when you look into your own eyes in the mirror. Do you like what you see, who you are and how you behave? And if you do something to disappoint yourself and others, can you recognise it, take ownership and grow?

In the words of my wise colleague, I want to remind you that: "You cannot please all of the people all of the time, only some of the people some of the time."

Some questions to think about.

1.   What were your biggest disappointments this year?

2. Where did you disappoint others?

3. What can you learn from this?

Courage to ask for support.

We all need support from each other at some point in time. But for some reason, we have this notion that if we ask for support, it is a sign of weakness. I do not know where this idea stems from, but for me, it takes courage for anyone to ask for help. To ask for support means that we are vulnerable, which may be an uncomfortable position for some of us. But being vulnerable is not a place of weakness. It takes immense bravery and courage to put up your hand to ask for what you need. If you flip your limiting belief around, from asking for support is a weakness, to asking for support takes courage, how might your relationships change? By asking, you allow others to support you. Most people will jump at the opportunity to add value to your life; to be your support crew and to feel valued in the process. Supporting each other is what keeps the world turning.

The story of fallen oaks.

My brother, who lives on a farm in Stellenbosch, a beautiful area in the Cape Winelands in South Africa, told me about all the big acorn trees that blew over on the farm after a huge, windy storm. To put this in context, I need you to imagine 30–50 m tall trees with lush green leaves and huge branches as thick as a human man. They are majestic and magical. I saw pictures of these magnificent, straight, beautiful, tall trees lying on the ground, almost as if a hurricane had passed through.

After seeing all the fallen giants, I realised that even though these tall, beautiful, flourishing trees looked strong and solid, they fell over because their ground support got soft, and the wind was giving out harsh blows. They fell over despite being majestic and strong.

The same applies to us. You can have the best background, morals, values, and work ethic. You can grow and flourish and have beautiful branches and leaves, but you may fall over without the support when the ground gets soft and the wind hands out harsh blows. Things will go wrong when you least expect it. You are not invincible even if you feel on top of the world. This is what makes you human!

In the end, however, it is not always possible to stay upright during a storm. It is more than okay to lean on support. Remember to lean on your support wall to rest and take a breath when you feel that you are hitting an emotional wall. It is important to ask for the support you need and deserve.

Think about your 3 biggest challenges at the moment:

1. What support might you need?

2. Who can support you with these challenges?

3. What does that support look like?

4. Who do you support and what does that look like?

You may be one of the lucky ones who have people in your life who will love and support you, no matter what. The whole you – with warts and all! If you don't, you may need to go and search for people or a community where that can be true for you. I like to call them your go-to-gang. Those people whose opinions matter most, who love and support you through the good and the bad.

Write down 3-5 people's names who you want in your go-to gang. The people in your corner or inner circle who you truly value.

Look at this page as a reminder the next time you have to make hard decisions or choices or ask for support. Ask only yourself and the people on this piece of paper what they think, and decide what pieces of advice resonate. If you struggle to fill the page, it may be an invitation to start connecting more with people and create relationships that really matter.

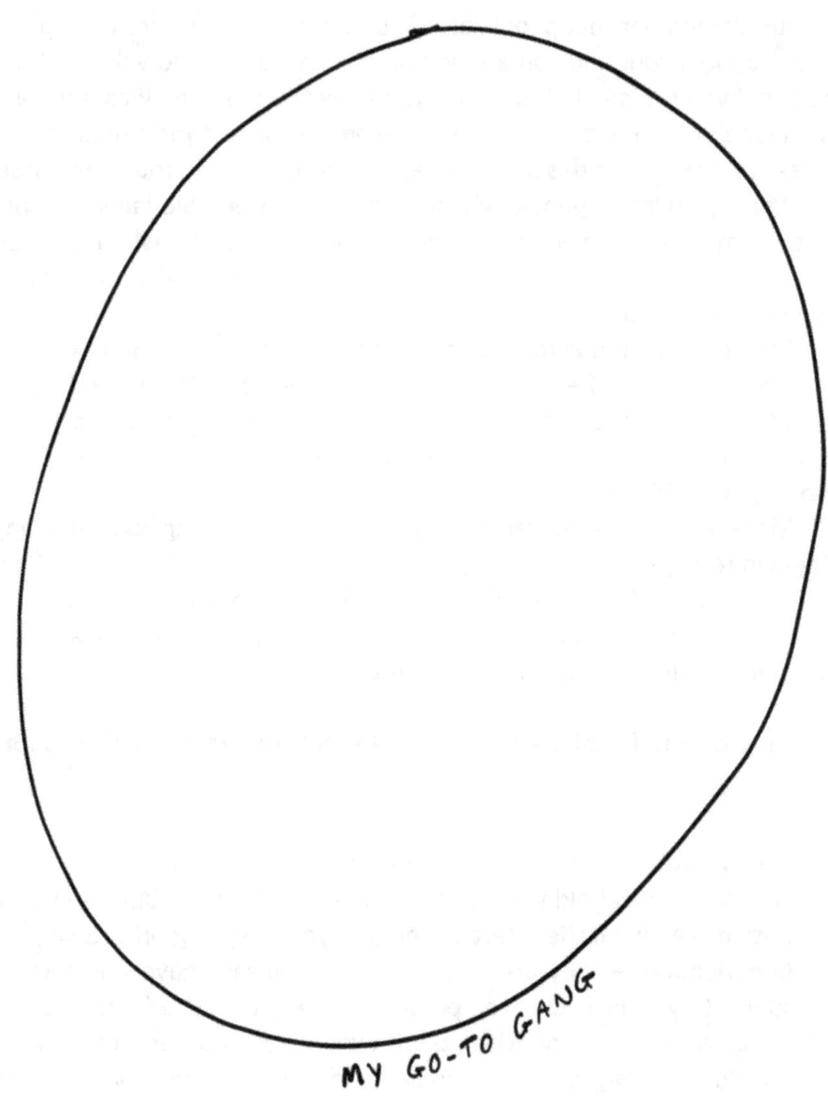

My go-to gang.

Just remember that people also find purpose when they can help. When they support you, find something that you can do to add value to them in return. Even the most minor thing can have the most significant impact on someone else. In this way, you also become a support for others. It is not a one-way street. And this is what keeps the world going around and around.

After speaking to people who have had a considerable fallout or conflict with someone, usually with someone close to them, when I probe, it surfaces that they assumed the other person knew what they needed, wanted, or expected. But they did not.

Be specific in asking for support: What you need, want, and expect from others. We are all different and may interpret support in different ways.

What does support look like for you? What type of support do you need from someone? Ask them and be clear and make agreements that are possible to achieve.

Make sure that they can supply what you are asking for. And support them in return.

You may also find different types of support from different people in your life. See if you can complete your support circle by allocating certain roles to specific people or what you wish for them to fulfil in your life.

Here is a brief explanation of the different roles in the circle of support:

Accountability partners – they are the people that reminds you about your why. They hold you accountable in a loving way, but also kick your butt into action if they start seeing that you are going off course.

Cheerleaders – they are the people that always have our back. That supports you in every way possible, who gets excited with you when things goes wrong and who sits with you when times are tough.

Mentors – they are the people who gives advice from a place of experience. They guide, teach and impart wisdom.

Colleagues – they are your peers. Working side by side usually understanding what you go through at work, daily.

Leaders – they are the people whose vision is clear and inspiring. Who coaches, support and help you grow as a person.

Recognise when you need support and then ask for what you need.

Support is grace and kindness wrapped in unconditional love.

Think about the different roles of people in your life and add their names in the circle of support.

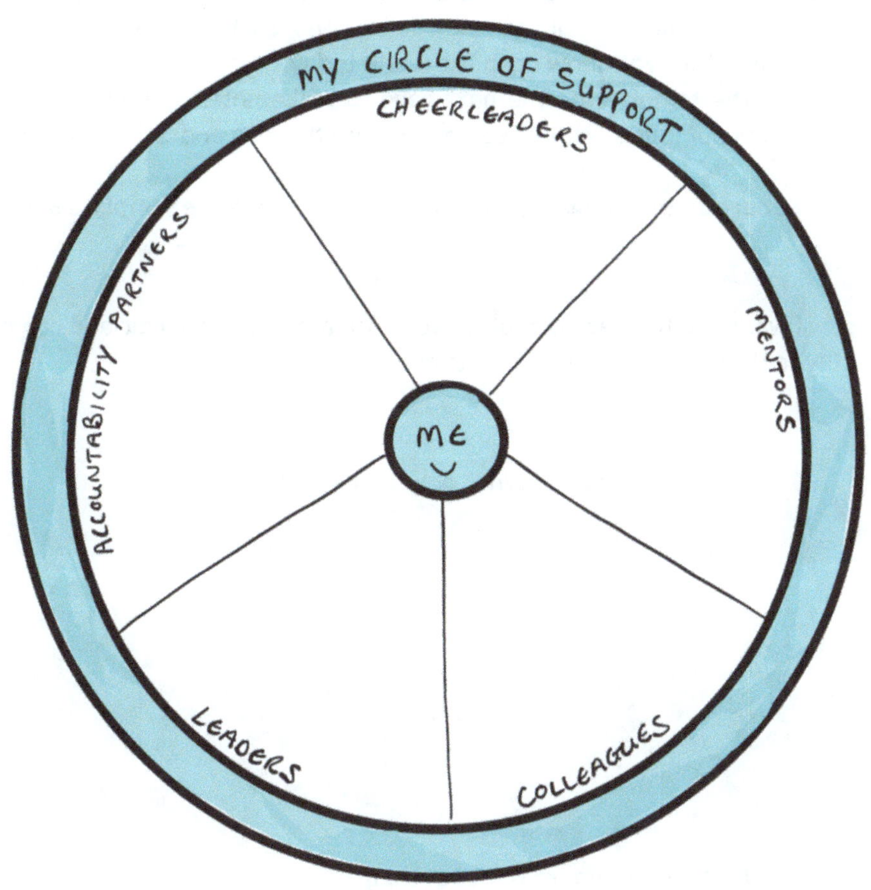

My support circle.

Me Time.

It is now time to reflect. Gratitude is such a wonderful thing. Take the time to pause and reflect on the people or influencers who may have influenced some parts of your life choices. Those who played a role in who you are or how you show up in the world today.
Use the template on the next page to make notes and add additional notes in your journal should you need more thinking and writing space.

Reflect on the following questions and complete the template below.

I want you to imagine a future you. You are having a picnic and can only invite three people as your guests of honour.

1. Who would I invite? Write down their names.

2. What do I admire most about them?

3. If I could ask them each one question, what would it be?

4. If I could tell them one thing that I am grateful for that they taught me that impacted me positively, what would it be?

If you are brave, I want to encourage you to write them each a letter, a WhatsApp or email and send it to them if you can. Don't wait. Tell them now what you discovered and what you see in them or how they have or continue to touch your life. They must know how you feel. I did it a couple of years ago and I am so glad I did, because the people who have impacted me the most and continue to do so, now know their impact. It is not only a gift to them but a gift to me. The practice of gratitude physically changes your brain and your life.

GUESTLIST	WHAT I ADMIRE	THE GIFTS & WISDOM
①	①	①
②	②	②
③	③	③

CHAPTER 16.

TIME CAPSULE.

When I was 17 years old, our family started a new chapter when we moved from Pretoria to Cape Town where my dad started a new job. An excellent opportunity for him and our family, but terrible timing for a young teenage girl still finding herself. I adapted as well as I could and made new friends fast, but it was not easy.

I felt honoured when I was shortlisted for the Learner Council after six months in my new school. As part of the voting process all candidates had to make a speech in the school hall in front of the whole school. I decided to do something different for my speech which was petrifying, by the way, and rather than the normal 'I will be a good Prefect' speech, I told this story, which I adapted for my speech.

There was once this man who went for a walk on the beach. The mist was extremely thick as it could get close to the sea. Through the mist he saw another man busy throwing something into the water ahead of him. He realised that hundreds of thousands of starfish washed up on the sand were dying. To save them, the man scooped up handfuls of starfish at a time and threw them back into the water. The man who went for his morning walk watched this and shook his head. As he got closer to the rescuer, he asked him: "Why are you doing this? It is an impossible task, and you can't save them all." The other man took a starfish into his hand, looked at him, and as he threw the starfish back into the ocean, he said: "I made a difference to that one, didn't I?"[32]

You may wonder why I shared this story? When my husband asked me why I wanted to write this book, I thought about it for a moment and said, "I wish I had known all of these things I have included in this book 20 years ago. I wonder how my life would have been different? How many more opportunities would I have seen? How many better choices would I have made? How much more value could I have added to myself and others?"

This story illustrates my wish so beautifully. I wrote this book hoping that I could also make a difference, even if only for one person.

The idea that I wish I had had all the knowledge and skills 20 years ago made me think of a time capsule.

As little girls, my best friend and I wrote messages that we put in old bottles or Eno medicine bottles - do you still remember those?, and dug holes in the garden to bury our messages. We wrote down our dreams, the adventures we still wanted to have, our stories and everything important to us then. We promised each other we would dig the bottles up again when we were older. We grew up, and I moved to Cape Town in later years – the time capsules but only a memory. When I spoke to my friend years later, she told me she could never find our buried treasures again. But I am sure someone will find our messages from the past one day. Our time capsules.

I am not the same person I was back then. I've grown. I've learned. I've changed for the better. I sometimes wonder about my future self. What will she be doing, saying, thinking? I am really the future me in the making.

Think about what you would put in your time capsule – the treasures you would share with your future self.

---

[32] "The Starfish Story – Original Story by: Loren Eisley." *Ataturk Society of America RSS*, http://www.ataturksociety.org/the-starfish-story-original-story-by-loren-eisley/.

* * *

Me Time.

It is now time to reflect. All the answers you seek you have. Take a moment to put together some of the discoveries you made during this life journey that will enable you to live the life you truly desire.
Use the template on the next page to make notes and add additional notes in your journal should you need more thinking and writing space.

Create your time capsule now.
Write a note to your future self - the 20 years from now version of you. In this message, I want you to remind your future self of the following things:

1.   The three things that I am grateful for.

2.   The three fresh beliefs about myself and others.

3. The three goals I have for myself.

4. The three wishes have for my life.

5. The three nuggets of wisdom I want to hold on to.

6. The three things people love about me.

7. The three really hard things that I face right now that might look a
    little less daunting from a future me perspective.

Once you are done with this time capsule message, record it on your
phone, wrap yourself in a blanket and play it. Let it sink in. Listen to your
own wise words. Feel what it feels like to become the person you are
supposed to be. Focus on your own path. Believe in the power of dreams.
Be grateful for the blessings all the way on this very special journey called
life.

GRATEFUL
VALUES
BELIEFS
GOALS
WISHES
WISDOM

CHAPTER 17.

TIME TO COMMIT TO YOU.

Have you ever heard the following phrases: 'the timing for that was off' or 'it was not the right time for us' or 'maybe next time'? Timing is an interesting phenomenon. But I would like to challenge this and ask: is it the timing that is right or not, or is it our mindset and choices that either play out positively or negatively? I believe that your focus and what you prioritise will determine your journey.

I saw a documentary on the life of the well-known F1 Grand Prix racer, Lewis Hamilton. His dad LOVED racing, so they spent a lot of time watching races together. When Lewis was young, they could not afford a new go-cart, so they bought a secondhand cart and built it up together. Lewis started to compete at a very young age. His dad exposed him to the racing world, and he cultivated the love, passion and talent of this young boy who is now a top racer in the world. I believe that when you are born into a family who have a passion for something, chances are that you will be exposed to this from a young age and the combination of talent and time spent may result in you being pretty good or at least have a passion for this talent. Whether it is sport, leisure, music, food – anything, really. What you are exposed to and where you choose to spend your time will have a very specific result. So, the question now is, where do you choose to spend your time and energy at this moment that you are truly passionate about?

Dreams will stay just dreams if you don't grab a hold of them.

We all have limiting beliefs or obstacles that life throws at us that stop us in our tracks. We start believing that we will never reach our dreams. That it is impossible. That we do not deserve it. That happiness is only for a select few. That love is not our thing or that we are not good enough, brave enough, skilled enough. And then we give up.

Sound familiar?

This is, however, utter bull! If you believe all that, you are right. It WILL be your reality! But if you focus on what you want most in life rather than what scares you most in life, you will open yourself up to the opportunities that come your way. You will have the right mindset to push yourself to be better. You will surround yourself with the people who will love you and become your biggest cheerleaders. Life is a mirror. It gives you not what you want, but what you need.

To have a vision or dream for yourself in life is a great motivator. It can instigate change, but it is not sustainable without intent, energy, mindfulness and conscious focus, action and choice.

Visionary focus will drive momentum, but consistent hard work is the key.

Any athlete will tell you that it starts with a vision followed by a lot of drive, self-discipline, determination, and guidance to win in the end. It does not happen by chance. What no one tells you is that consistency is the key. The best athletes in the world have talent and drive yes, but what sets them apart is their commitment to do the work. They put in the hours, the sweat and the tears. Every single day. What you focus on is who you will become.

Get ready to shift your self-talk.

How you speak to yourself and others has a significant impact on your state, mindset, influence, and impact. Listen to yourself when you speak to yourself and the people around you. Are the words you use empowering or disempowering? Positive or negative? Open for possibilities or closed for possibilities? I can, or I can't? Is it a problem, or is it an opportunity?

Setting intentions is a way to manage your focus, so think about the following questions for a moment:

1. What are you focusing on in your life today?

2. What attitude and mindset are you choosing?

3. What might you be missing that is right in front of you?

The power of focus.

I remember when I got a small Hyundai Getz. It was a little red car and once I started to drive around, I was amazed at how many red Getzes there were on the roads that I had never noticed before. The same applied when I was pregnant. I suddenly saw so many pregnant women wherever I went. This is called selective focus. Whatever you focus on, you will see or attract. The same applies to everything in life. One of my previous bosses used to say: "You will get what you desire the most in life and what you fear the most in life." At the time, I did not understand this, but she was right. If you focus on the things you want most in life, you will see the opportunities, and focus and energy will ensure that you find a way to make your dreams come true. The same applies to the negative. If you are always focusing on the negative, the chances are that you will attract the negative towards you. Some people call this the 'law of attraction'.

Athletes understand this exceptionally well. That is why good athletes visualise themselves running and winning, jumping higher than the pole, jumping further than the record. They feel what it would feel like in their mind's eye. They understand the power of focus and positive thinking. In their mind's eye they've already won. They focus on that feeling and not the sense of possible defeat. Their bodies will follow their thoughts. They may seem arrogant to some, but it is not arrogance. It is a winner mindset. If they don't believe that they will win and make you think it, they will not make the cut.

This made me think of the time when my elder son was seven and participated in a mathematics competition. He passed the first and second rounds and got through to the finals. I was a bit nervous for him, but he was confident. On our way to the final round, he said to me: "Mom, I am going to win." and as a mother who wants to protect her son, I said: "Whatever happens, I am so proud of you, and it does not matter if you win or not." I wanted to soften the blow if he didn't win. But in his mind, it was a done deal. He had complete confidence in his ability, and he wanted it. There was no doubt whatsoever. And he did – he won. Since then, I have never second-guessed him. He focused on the win. I focused on the potential failure. In her book *Battle Hymn of the Tiger Mother*, Amy Chua refers to 'parents assuming strength, not fragility'. As a parent, this is profound because when we are 'protecting' our kids with the best intent, we presume that they are fragile, but we should instead assume, focus on and encourage their strength.

Setting your intentions daily will keep the focus and momentum.

I used to get out of bed worried, tired, and not always looking forward to a busy day. My attitude was an attitude of survival and just getting through another day. I was on autopilot most of the time. I am also not proud of this, but I became a functional mom. Focusing on getting the kids fed, dressed, and dropped off at school on time. But was this enough? Was it fair to them or me?

I realised that waking up in the morning is a gift. Seeing the sun come up is spectacular. Having time for myself early in the morning before everyone wakes up, to write this book or meditate or exercise, is a blessing. Now I choose my state right at the beginning of the morning. Will my attitude be positive or negative? Is life happening to me or for me? Are problems a stumbling block or an opportunity? I choose gratitude, connection, love, and growth. I open myself up for possibilities and because I focus on it, I attract it. And it is contagious! It influences my kids, husband, and everyone I deal with during the day. And it helps me cope when things do go wrong or not as planned.

Someone once said to me: "Don't fake it until you make it, fake it until you become it." And this is true. Set your intentions for the day. Be clear about what kind of day you want. Don't get derailed by situations or people. Remind yourself why you are doing what you are doing. And if by chance you have a miserable day, acknowledge how you feel and why, and try again tomorrow. Every day will have challenges, but even in the challenges there are lessons and learnings – it is up to you if you are open to receive it.

Life is a journey.

What if I told you that everything you dream about is already yours. It is yours to dream. To imagine. To want more than anything. And to make your own. The only thing standing between you and your dreams is you. Getting out of your own way is possible. Imagine that this is all possible. See yourself and how far you've come. Say thank you to yourself and the people who helped you on your journey. Life is the journey – don't miss the journey by only focusing on the destination. Ask yourself, in six months from now, will you be celebrating your progress or be making excuses – the choice is really yours!

* * *

Me time.

It is now time to reflect. All the answers you seek you already have. Take a moment to put together some of the discoveries you made during this life journey that will enable you to live the life you truly desire.

Use the template on the next page to make notes and add additional notes in your journal should you need more thinking and writing space.

Let's do a practical exercise and answer the following questions for yourself.

1.   What do I prioritise daily?

2.   What am I grateful for?

3.   What is my reason for being? My life purpose? Most people know what they do and how they do it, but not why they do it.

4. What am I saying yes to in my life?

5. What am I saying no to in my life?

6. How would I like to show up in life?

7. What do I really want to do, to be, to feel?

8. What are the commitments I am making to me in this moment that I will honour?

9. What is one action I will take starting today to get me closer to my goal? Remember to schedule it – otherwise it will never happen!

MY COMMITMENT TO ME!

①

②

③

IV.

CONCLUSION.

We've come to the end of a beautiful journey. Thank you for making the time for you. I started the book by saying that we would cover the following areas. I hope you found what you needed. You started this journey with an assessment. Assess where you are now in terms of taking ownership of how you want to show up in life:

A – assess where you are now and where you want to be and focus on the right things
B – believe that you can
O – out with the old beliefs, in with the fresh beliefs
U – understand your why and why not
T – think about who you are and how you want to show up in this world
T – take ownership of your life
I – include the people and things that give you joy
M – make it happen
E – embrace every moment.

Rate yourself again from 1-5 for each area, where 1 is not good and 5 is fantastic. Circle your answer.

1. How happy am I with my life today?

1.   2.   3.   4.   5.

2. Am I focusing on what will bring me closer to living my desired life?

1.   2.   3.   4.   5.

3. How confident do I feel that I will reach my dreams?

1.   2.   3.   4.   5.

4. How open am I to changing the beliefs that keeps me away from my dreams?

1.   2.   3.   4.   5.

5. I know and understand my purpose in life

1.   2.   3.   4.   5.

6. I know who I am and how I want to show up in this world

1.   2.   3.   4.   5.

7. I allow others to prioritise what I achieve or don't achieve in life

1.   2.   3.   4.   5.

8. I have people in my life that brings me joy

1.   2.   3.   4.   5.

9. I make things happen and own my own happiness

1.   2.   3.   4.   5.

10. I embrace every moment and make the most of it – in good times and bad times

1.   2.   3.   4.   5.

Compare this rating to the rating you did right at the beginning of this book. What shifted for you?
Remember to continue doing your work. Keep growing. Keep the momentum going.

It's about time for you to shine!

* * *

This book was a discovery of you. And about the real moments that matter. A reminder that it is your time to shine.

I wish I had read a book like this when I was younger. I am incredibly grateful to all the people who have and are still informing my own experiences, learning and growth.

I took my learning, experience and interpretation of many different people's ideas, conversations and thoughts and tried to make sense of them for myself.

I want to thank you for taking the time for yourself. Take out of this selection of thoughts, insights, stories and learning what you need. Make this your own and apply what you've discovered in the way that works best for you.

My wish for you is that it will add value to your life and the lives of others. Please share what you've learned and pay it forward. If you had told me five years ago that I would write a book and do my own drawings, I would have laughed at you. Never say never. Something I learned along the way is that pressure can either create diamonds or burst pipes. I wish you just the right amount of pressure to create diamonds in your life!

In the wise words of Yoda: "Do or do not. There is no try."[33]

It's about time.

What do you choose?

-THE END -
(or is it the beginning?) ...

---

[33] Shine (2018). *8 Powerful Quotes From Yoda, the OG Wellness Guru.* [online] Thrive Global. Available at: https://medium.com/thrive-global/8-powerful-quotes-from-yoda-the-og-wellness-guru-ce03db397749.

NOTES.

CHAPTER 1 - BECOME A MASTER OF TIME.

[1] Sive.rs. 2009. *The Time Paradox – by Philip Zimbardo and John Boyd | Derek Sivers*. [online] Available at: <https://sive.rs/book/TimeParadox>.

[2] Snyder, C., Lopez, S., Edwards, L. and Marques, S., 2021. *The Oxford Handbook of Positive Psychology*. Oxford: Oxford University Press USA - OSO, pp.195-203.

[3] Manzella, K., 2022. *Kintsugi – Art of Repair | Traditional Kyoto*. [online] Traditionalkyoto.com. Available at: <https://traditionalkyoto.com/culture/kintsugi/>.

[4] 2022. *Discrete emotion theory* [online] Wikipedia. Available at: https://en.wikipedia.org/wiki/Discrete_emotion_theory

CHAPTER 2 - HOW STORIES CAN LIMIT AND EXPAND US.

[5] Wikipedia Contributors, 2019. *Diamond Sutra*. [online]. Wikipedia. Available at: <https://en.wikipedia.org/wiki/Diamond_Sutra>.

[6] Ayan, S., 2018. *The Brain's Autopilot Mechanism Steers Consciousness*. [online] Scientific American. Available at: <https://www.scientificamerican.com/article/the-brains-autopilot-mechanism-steers-consciousness/>.

[7] Lightbody, C., 2020. *Are we wired for stories*.

[8] 2022. [online] Available at: <https://dictionary.cambridge.org/dictionary/english/assumption>.

[9] 2010. *The power of connection*. [video] Available at: <https://www.youtube.com/watch?v=HEaERAnIqsY>.

CHAPTER 4 - TIME TO UNCOVER WHAT GIVES YOU JOY.

[10] What I Learned While Making a Movie About Happiness, 2013. *What I Learned While Making a Movie About Happiness*. [video] Available at: <https://www.youtube.com/watch?v=sM_xtk8aqh0>.

[11] Conklin, D., 2013. *The Role of the Brain in Happiness*. [online] Psychology Today. Available at: <https://www.psychologytoday.com/us/blog/in-the-face-adversity/201302/the-role- the-brain-in-happiness>.

[12] 2013. An Experiment in Gratitude | The Science of Happiness. [video] Available at: <https://www.youtube.com/watch?v=oHv6vTKD6lg>.

[13] Laughteryoga.org. 2021. *Laughter Yoga International - Health, Happiness and World Peace*. [online] Available at: <https://laughteryoga.org>.
[14] *Lung volumes*. (n.d.). Https://Www.Physio-Pedia.Com/Lung_Volumes. Retrieved 2021, from https://www.physio-pedia.com/Lung_Volumes.
[15] Louwman, R. C. (2021, January 29). Happiness. Personal.

CHAPTER 5 - TIME TO LEAN INTO FEAR.
[16] Gilbert, E. (2016). Courage: The Road Trip. In *Big magic* (pp. 25–27). essay, Penguin USA.
[17] Fear by Kahlil Gibran - Your daily poem. (n.d.). Retrieved April 5, 2022, from http://www.yourdailypoem.com/listpoem.jsp?poem_id=3608
[18] *Fear*. Cambridge Dictionary. (n.d.). Retrieved April 5, 2021, from https://dictionary.cambridge.org/dictionary/english/fear
[19] Vujicic, N. (n.d.). *Nick Vujicic*. Nick Vujicic: Fear is often described as False Evidence Appearing Real, Retrieved April 5, 2021, from https://whatsmyquote.com/quote/fear-is-often-described-as-false-evidence-appearing-real/page/4
[20] Erasmus, K. (2017, September 12). Understanding Fear. Personal.
[21] Stramrood, R. (2017, September 13). Pushing through fear. Personal.

CHAPTER 8 - TIME TO RELOOK YOUR BELIEFS.
[22] HarperCollins Publishers Ltd. (n.d.). *Belief definition and meaning: Collins English Dictionary*. Belief definition and meaning | Collins English Dictionary. Retrieved April 5, 2022, from https://www.collinsdictionary.com/dictionary/english/belief

CHAPTER 10 - TIME TO PRIORITISE.
[23] Burfoot, Amby. "The 10-Percent Rule." *Runner's World*, Runner's World, 3 Mar. 2022, https://www.runnersworld.com/training/a20781512/the-10-percent-rule/.
[24] Benjamin Wedro, MD. "It Band Syndrome Treatment, Symptoms, Recovery Time." *MedicineNet*, MedicineNet, 4 Mar. 2022, https://www.medicinenet.com/iliotibial_band_syndrome/article.htm.
[25] Admin. "Why It Takes a Decade of Training to Be a Head Sushi Chef." *Kobe Jones*, 14 Mar. 2017, https://www.kobejones.com.au/why-it-takes-a-decade-of-training-to-be-a-head-sushi-chef/.
[26] "Bento Boxes: Kids Web Japan." *Web Japan*, https://web-japan.org/kidsweb/virtual/bento/bento04.html.

CHAPTER 12 - TIME TO HATCH SOME HABITS.

[27] Sylvester, Brad. "Fact Check: Did Aristotle Say, 'We Are What We Repeatedly Do'?" *Check Your Fact*, Check Your Fact, 26 June 2019, https://checkyourfact.com/2019/06/26/fact-check-aristotle-excellence-habit-repeatedly-do/.

CHAPTER 13 - TIME TO GROW AND LET GO – OWN MY IMPACT.

[28] Schroeder, Audra. "What Is the 'Two Guys on a Bus' Meme?" *The Daily Dot*, 23 Nov. 2021, https://www.dailydot.com/unclick/two-guys-on-a-bus-meme/.

[29] "How to Sleep Better." *MasterClass*, MasterClass, 18 Mar. 2022, https://www.masterclass.com/classes/matthew-walker-teaches-the-science-of-better-sleep/chapters/how-to-sleep-better?utm_source%3DEmail.

[30] Makin, Simon. "Deep Sleep Gives Your Brain a Deep Clean." *Scientific American*, Scientific American, 1 Nov. 2019, https://www.scientificamerican.com/article/deep-sleep-gives-your-brain-a-deep-clean1/.

CHAPTER 15 -TIME FOR SUPPORT.

[31] KLINE, NANCY. *Time to Think: Listening to Ignite the Human Mind.* CASSELL, 2021.

CHAPTER 16 - TIME CAPSULE.

[32] "The Starfish Story – Original Story by: Loren Eisley." *Ataturk Society of America RSS*, http://www.ataturksociety.org/the-starfish-story-original-story-by-loren-eisley/.

CONCLUSION.

[33] Shine (2018). *8 Powerful Quotes From Yoda, the OG Wellness Guru.* [online] Thrive Global. Available at: https://medium.com/thrive-global/8-powerful-quotes-from-yoda-the-og-wellness-guru-ce03db397749.

ABOUT THE AUTHOR.

Co-Active Coach, Facilitator and
Customer and Employee Experience Designer.

My mission is to make the world a more kind, honest, open and passionate place. I see myself as that warm hug that supports, comforts and celebrates with people on a journey to uncover, reconnect and unleash their superpowers – even those who don't like hugs!

https://www.linkedin.com/in/mareli